P9-CFT-102

400

7-7

101 WAYS
TO
GENERATE
GREAT
IDEAS

101 WAYS
TO
GENERATE
GREAT
IDEAS

Timothy R V Foster

**KOGAN
PAGE**

For Christopher, Lauren, Tiffany and Stephanie – four great ideas

First published in 1991

Apart from any fair dealing for the purposes of research or private study, or criticism or review, as permitted under the Copyright, Designs and Patents Act, 1988, this publication may only be reproduced, stored or transmitted, in any form or by any means, with the prior permission in writing of the publishers, or in the case or reprographic reproduction in accordance with the terms of licences issued by the Copyright Licensing Agency. Enquiries concerning reproduction outside those terms should be sent to the publishers at the undermentioned address:

Kogan Page Limited
120 Pentonville Road
London N1 9JN

© Timothy R V Foster

British Library Cataloguing in Publication Data

A CIP record for this book is available from the British Library.

ISBN 0-7494-0533-3

Typeset by Saxon Printing Limited, Derby
Printed and bound in Great Britain by Clays Ltd, St Ives plc

Contents

Introduction

Many people think that ideas just happen. Look at the scripts:

'Hey, I just had a great idea!'
'That gives me an idea!'
'How's this for an idea?'

Well, of course, ideas do just happen. Yet we can't rely on happenstance. Don't we really spend our lives running to *these* scripts?

'What we need is a really good idea to solve this problem.'
'Has anybody got any ideas?'
'I wish I had some idea of how to deal with this!'
'There has to be a way!'

We need to be able to obtain great ideas *on demand*. This book is about *generating* great ideas – not about having them *happen* to you. It is *proactive* rather than *reactive*.

By following the concepts in these pages, you will find it much easier to generate great ideas – *when you need them*.

My dictionary defines *idea*, among other things, as a thought; mental conception; mental image; notion; plan; scheme; project; intention; aim; design. These are the meanings I intend in this book. (It also defines the word as a hazy perception; vague impression; fanciful notion; fancy; inkling – these are interim conditions you are allowed to occupy on your way to greatness.) Oh, yes, it defines *great* as much higher in some quality or degree; much above the ordinary or average. And to *generate* is defined as to bring into being; cause to be; produce; originate.

So how do we go about generating great ideas? It's a *process*. There are steps to take, procedures to follow. In this book the concepts are organised as follows:

- Understanding problems
- Understanding the mind
- Building your own creativity
- Generating ideas in groups
- Techniques to develop solutions
- Techniques to measure ideas.

How to Get the Most out of This Book

The 101 ways that are outlined here are real, based on real experiences. All the anecdotes really happened. There's no fluff to pad the book out. It's intentionally lean, to give you fast solutions to problems that you may have.

The mechanisms described here are not intended to be rigid rules. They are meant to be idea prompters. Allow yourself to apply variations as you see fit.

Start by reading the book through, from front to back. That shouldn't take you much more than an hour. Have a pencil or highlighter to hand. When you come across a way that seems to be useful, circle it. Dog-ear the page. Then go back and see if you can adapt those ideas to your way of doing business. Use them as a launching pad. Some of the ideas may appear familiar to you. Fine. They are there for completeness, so you don't miss anything. I guarantee that some of the concepts will be new to you, and I hope you find these helpful in bringing you the success you so richly deserve.

In the back of the book, you'll find a reading list and a comprehensive index.

Understanding Problems

Why do you need to generate great ideas? To solve *problems*. 'Necessity is the mother of invention.' The trouble is, quite often we find ourselves chasing the wrong problem – barking up the wrong tree – spinning our wheels – grasping the wrong end of the stick, you know what I mean?

What we need is a very clear understanding of what the *real problem* is. On the next few pages, you will find a series of ways to develop this.

Way 1 Define the current situation

The first step you must take in generating great ideas is have a clear understanding of where you are now. To make any journey, it's always helpful to know your starting point. Write it out. If you don't use a computer, use 3 × 5 inch index cards. This will make it easier to shift things around later. If you're working with a group of people, use a flipchart and stick the pages on the walls of the room.

When you're defining your present situation, use as many different measurement devices as you can (put each one on a separate card or sheet). You could use the following headings, for example:

- Background
- Need
- Geographical/Physical location
- Time parameters
- Competitive position
- Financial position
- Resources available
- Resources not available

Let me give you an example of how this works. In 1982 I was doing some freelance work for a New York advertising agency, and one of their accounts was Granby Aircraft Corporation, of Texas (I've changed the name). Granby made a pair of very appealing, highly efficient four-seater private aeroplanes. A few years earlier, I had written *The Aircraft Owner's Handbook – Everything You Need To Know About Buying, Operating and Selling an Aircraft*. This had made me into some kind of expert – a regular aircraft-ownership maven. Now the problem facing Granby was that sales of their $120,000 'Porsche of the skies' were very slow – less than 100 units for the year as against over 400 in their best year, maybe

36 months earlier. This was largely attributable to the state of the economy, and soaring costs, particularly fuel. Bruce Friedlich, the agency president, asked me if I could come up with some ideas for Granby. The idea was, if I did, I'd get to work on the account. And if I didn't, they'd lose the account.

Since I was spending most of my time writing about financial services, and my first love was aviation, you can imagine how appealing the challenge was!

Basically I had a week. I applied the concept outlined above.

- *Background.* Granby produce two fast four-seater single-engine private aircraft, the 400 and the 500. They have an excellent image, particularly of efficiency and quality, since the line was substantially modernised and upgraded a few years earlier. Yet sales have plummeted from about 400 a year to about 100. This is not a Granby-only problem – the whole general aviation industry is on the ropes. Granby are first or second in sales each month in their class of high-performance single-engine four-seaters.

  Granbys are bought almost exclusively by business people – mostly men – to fly themselves. Utilisation is more for business than leisure travel. It is not an aeroplane for the first-time buyer. For a person to learn to fly in a Granby is very rare. A Granby owner has usually been flying a few years, and is moving up to something more sophisticated when the purchase is made.

- *Need.* A big idea for Granby that could help to increase sales, demonstrate continued leadership, be implemented swiftly and not cost a lot of money.

- *Geography.* Granby are in Texas. They have dealers all over the USA, and to a limited extent, throughout the world (export sales are very low). I am in New York (about five hours' travel time).

- *Time.* ASAP – I need the main concepts this week. We should be able to implement the idea within a couple of months.
- *Competitive position.* The Granby is a superior product, reasonably priced. It offers high speed and incredible fuel efficiency (18 miles to the gallon at 180 mph!). All aircraft manufacturers are in a sales slump.
- *Financial position.* If the trend is not reversed, the Granby company's owners, a conglomerate, could pull the plug. We have a very low budget.
- *Resources available.* Receptive audience, loyal base of 4500 Granby owners; supportive aviation media. Demonstrator aircraft are available for use in activities. Open-minded management.
- *Resources* not *available.* Lots of money. Lots of time.

So that's the sort of set-up that helps you to get going. We'll return to this case again and again as we progress and see how the process builds up.

Way 2 Define the goal, and make it measurable

What are you trying to achieve? Where are you trying to go? Where do you want to be when you've got there? How will you know you've made it? It's all very well to make some broad statement like: to solve world hunger; to reduce traffic congestion in London; to combat the threat of terrorism; to sell more soap; to be the leader of the pack. Objectives are important, *and* they must be measurable.

Going back to our Granby example, our goal was to evolve a promotional concept that would increase sales and maintain Granby's position of leadership. Yet those are the kinds of wishy-washy statement we must avoid. How do you measure those objectives? They should be stated in terms that can be tracked – to increase sales by 10 per cent, for example, with Granby developing a leading share of market, as measured by monthly reports from the General Aviation Manufacturers Association. Another way is to measure response to advertising or mailings, and the extent and tone of stories that develop in the specialist aviation media.

Way 3 Identify the gaps

Now that you know where you are and where you want to go, the next step is to identify the gaps between your present position and your desired one. Let's go back to our analysis of Granby and check them out:

- *Background gap.* The industry is in a bad way. Customers are staying away in droves, in spite of product excellence.
- *Needs gap.* A way to make effective promotional noise, increase sales and market share.
- *Geography gap.* Must spend a lot of time in Texas from my base in New York.
- *Time gap.* Must go to it *now!*
- *Competitive gap.* None better.
- *Financial gap.* Whatever we do can't cost much. I think our budget was about $180,000, which for a national US campaign is peanuts.
- *Resource gaps.* Money and time.

An understanding of these gaps helps you with the next step.

Way 4 Identify the core problem you are trying to solve

A lot of people waste a lot of time trying to generate solutions to problems, only to find they have been chasing the wrong problem. How can you identify the *right* problem? Well, how about using a process of elimination? Make a list of potential problem areas, and then indicate for each one whether you have a problem there or not. Then analyse the results. Let's stay with our Granby example. Sales are down. That's not the core problem. *Why* are they down?

Area	Problem	No problem
Aircraft price $120,000	Doubled in last five years	–
Fuel cost $1.20 per gallon	Doubled in last five years	*But* 18 mpg at 180 mph! (Best of all)
Other operating costs	All increased heavily, more than inflation	–
Quality of product	–	Excellent and upgraded
Dealer network	Some weakness	In place and running
Delivery time	–	No waiting
Functionality of product	–	Does its job very well
Image of product	Reputation for lack of room – has been made roomier	Good – perhaps a bit 'culty' – a flying Porsche
Safety record	–	Excellent One-piece wing for great strength
Owner satisfaction	–	Very high
Competition	–	Nothing to beat it at the price
Existing advertising	Limited coverage due to budgets	–
Media reports	–	All very positive

So, looking at the above table, what is the *real* problem we need to address? It's not a quality or delivery problem that has resulted in low sales. The Granby doesn't seem to have any competition to speak of. The media love the aircraft, so do its current owners; although there is a bit of a cult feeling to it, that could be an advantage. It's often been described as a flying Porsche – what red-blooded pilot wouldn't want that image? And Porsches aren't famous for room either (actually the current Granby has plenty of room, yet old perceptions are hard to kill). An increase in advertising spend, *per se*, would not do much for sales. There is some weakness in the dealer network, brought about by the generally poor sales picture. But fixing that isn't going to change things much.

So what is the problem? The answer is it costs too much. Too much to buy, too much to run. All aeroplanes cost too much. The cost of owning and operating an aeroplane had increased substantially more than inflation in the previous five years. So people who just had to fly were buying used aircraft, for which there was a fairly healthy market.

How could we get the costs down? Granby can hardly reduce its price by much. The price of fuel will probably only increase, not decrease. The other operating costs – insurance, maintenance, storage – they're not coming down. Yet the only thing that would boost sales would be a reduction in cost. So that was the real problem. How could we get the cost of buying and owning a Granby down enough to reverse the sales downtrend? We needed a *big* cut.

Way 5 Identify the audiences/users/ beneficiaries

Another step that must be carried out early in your analysis of the problem or challenge is to clearly understand to whom you should be talking. In our Granby example it would be:

- Granby aircraft owners
- Granby dealers
- Current other-brand aircraft owners
- Licensed pilots, potential owners
- New pilots, potential owners
- The aviation media (as influencers/endorsers)
- Granby employees (as stakeholders).

All these people are easily identifiable by name and address. In the USA, there were about 4500 Granby owners, maybe 30 Granby dealers and 200,000 current aircraft owners (this could be substantially reduced by aiming at owners of certain types of planes that would be suitable trade-ins for a Granby). Non-US audiences were not immediately targeted, due to budget limitations. Many of them would be reached through spillover from US activities, especially in Canada.

The aviation media consist of perhaps ten publications. Note that we were not aiming at non-pilots at all. Granby's story has limited appeal to someone who isn't already sold on flying, and who hasn't gone far enough into it to at least get a pilot's licence.

Granby employees were important as an audience, because we would want to keep their morale high by showing them something is happening – it's not all bad news.

In a different situation, you might want to look at high-volume or low-volume users and decision-makers in your field of interest, or people in the purchasing department, managing directors of companies, doctors, accountants, town councillors or the police. Perhaps some people need to be considered not because they buy or use the product or service, but because they can influence users, or influence legislation, or because they are part of your constituencies: employees, families of employees, the community, suppliers, trade customers and so on. Identifying and understanding what these categories are is an important step in developing your ideas.

Way 6 Do some research

There is a lot of information out there, just waiting to be useful for you. You can go to libraries and search through:

- Directories
- Reference books
- Encyclopedias
- Almanacs
- Atlases
- Dictionaries
- Biographies
- Newspapers
- Magazines

The librarian will help you. They can do computer and microfiche searches for you to identify books on particular subjects. There are also useful specialist libraries. I made a video called *Wheels – The Joy of Cars*, which was an assembly of a variety of interesting footage from newsreels and other film archives over the years. One bit featured the Royal Automobile Club (RAC) vintage-car London-to-Brighton rally of about 20 years earlier. I wanted to identify the various ancient vehicles, and all I had to go on was their rally number and a vague description (red, open top, two seats). I telephoned the RAC library. The librarian pulled out the original rally programme, I read him the cars' numbers and soon had the identifications I needed.

There are computer databases that can be searched. These will look for abstracts from published articles for example (eg *Textline*). You enter a few key words and give the computer a time frame and list of publications, and in a few moments you can have a printout of the various story headlines, or even the full text. Public relations and advertising agencies subscribe to this sort of service. If you have your own computer and a modem, you can tap into databases yourself through various computer utilities such as *Compuserve*.

Or maybe you do some original research. This can help you drive your whole programme. On the Granby Aircraft situation, we did a mailing to all Granby owners to find out a whole raft of things – why they bought the aeroplane (efficiency, performance), did they intend to buy another Granby (yes/no), what sort of flying they did (long trips, short trips, business, holidays, training) age groups, occupations – even things like ownership of video-cassette recorders (VCRs). In those days, US VCR ownership was about 25 per cent. I surmised that Granby owners, being techies and gadget freaks, would be more likely to own VCRs than plain non-plane folk. Correct: penetration was closer to 50 per cent. One idea was to use video to build the relationship with Granby owners. I wanted eventually to put the owner's manual and some advanced training material on video.

We started with a video called *The Granby Experience*. This was a film designed to make a Granby owner salivate, and want desperately to show it to his friends. It featured some beautiful footage that demonstrated the core concept of the Granby – its aerodynamic efficiency.

We sold 600 copies of this tape to Granby owners through the mail and invited them to show it to their friends and bring potential customers into the showrooms. We promised them a $1000 bounty if a plane was sold as a result. Three new Granbys (over $360,000 worth of aeroplanes) thus moved out of the hangars in the next couple of months. All from a little research carried out to confirm an idea.

Way 7 Hold a focus group

This is where you get groups of people together in a controlled environment and conduct an in-depth enquiry into your challenge. This process is quite expensive, compared to making a few phone calls or sending out questionnaires, but if it is done properly it's well worth while.

Typically, the focus group is conducted by a specialist company. They may even have specially designed premises to do the job. I went to one in my Merrill Lynch days when we were designing a new financial service, and we had ten investors in a room for four hours. They didn't know who the client was. We were watching from behind one-way glass, and the whole process was videotaped. Very eerie and very helpful.

You can use a focus group to identify perceived problems with your approach. You can show them your advertising or your commercial, or a write-up of the service, or a mock-up of the product. Skilfully handled, you can get a lot of information and a better understanding of your customer very quickly. By holding several focus groups with different types of people: heavy users, light users, non-users, men, women, doctors, airline pilots, mothers, mothers with teenage daughters, teenagers, etc, you can *focus* on the information you need to develop. You can also conduct them regionally: north, south, urban, rural, seaside, inland, French, German, multinational, and so on.

The secret of good focus groups is to have the right people in the group (the focus group firm *must* know how to find these) and have it run by an experienced facilitator who really understands what you want to achieve. Many words spoken by participants in a focus group have ended up as great advertising copy. You can't make up the kind of stuff you get from a focus group. It's too real.

Holding a focus group is a good way to identify or confirm the core problem you need to solve.

Way 8 Do a SWOT analysis

Another way of looking at the situation is to do a SWOT analysis. SWOT stands for Strengths, Weaknesses, Opportunities, Threats. Make a heading for each word and start identifying the appropriate items in each category. Ideally, you should do this with a group of people, using a large flipchart or wallboard. Let the items come up at random, allocating them where they belong. Let's look at our Granby example:

Strengths

- High-quality, good looking aeroplane
- Strongly built – excellent safety record
- Very efficient (18 mpg at 180 mph)
- Fast, good long-range performance – it does the job
- Very well equipped with desirable extras (radios, autopilot, etc)
- Porsche image, great heritage
- Fun to fly
- Available now, no waiting list
- Granby owners love the aircraft
- Strong, well-run owners' club

Weaknesses

- Expensive to buy and run compared to recent years (but not any more than the market-place)
- Not enough money for a major advertising/promotion campaign

Opportunities

- To find some way to lower the cost of ownership
- To use existing owners as ambassadors and recommenders
- To provide dealers with more traffic, make them healthier
- Increased sales would help to keep prices steady or reduce them
- Better corporate financial performance could attract additional investment for new product development

Threats

- Production rates could decline to such an extent that prices must be increased further
- Continued poor sales could reduce scope of dealer network, affecting service capability
- If something isn't done soon, company could go out of business, parent company could shut it down, or liquidate company
- Other possible aircraft-manufacturer failures could have domino effect on Granby or vice versa
- A very successful solution might create future delivery problems, since the company is currently only building about eight to ten aircraft a month

You'll notice that the SWOT technique works quite nicely at helping you zero in on the core problem – and even helps to suggest the direction of possible solutions.

Way 9 Write a description of the task

The act of writing a lucid description of a task will, in itself, help to clarify the points that need to be made and can often bring a fresh understanding of the problem.

The discipline of laying out the key aspects in a logical order will help to identify gaps. Even if you are writing it just for yourself or your team, avoid jargon, and don't assume a lot of prior knowledge. I have found it useful to have a basic format to follow when creating such a document. You don't have to be rigid about it. Here it is:

- *Purpose of document*
  An overview of the problem and the solution proposed or needed in no more than one or two paragraphs
- *Situation*
  The core facts of where we are right now
- *Background*
  Any relevant information that supports the situation:
  - Competitive, legislative, economic, historic, problems
- *Considerations*
  Aspects that must be considered in evolving a solution
  - Timing
  - Finance
  - Capabilities
  - Available or needed resources
- *Audiences*
  Who are impacted by the result or at whom the result is aimed
- *Objectives*
  What it is you're intending to achieve
- *Strategy*
  By what means you intend to achieve it
- *Tactics*
  Examples of solutions
- *Discussion* (optional)
  A brief review of the pros and cons of different courses of action
  Rejected approaches and why they were dropped.

Way 10 Explain the problem to a six-year-old, and vice versa

By now, if you've used some of the techniques described here, you should have a fairly good idea of the problem you are trying to solve. To get it absolutely clear, find a friendly six-year-old and try explaining the problem. Your objective here is to do such a good job, that you can get the child to explain it back to you.

Listen very carefully to the words that come back (a tape recorder is a good idea here). You may be surprised at the insights that a mind untrammelled by preconceptions can produce. I explained the Granby situation to my son, Christopher (seven). Then he dealt it back to me, pretty accurately. 'So what's the problem?' I asked. 'Well, it costs too much money!' he replied.

Here's the problem for Granby. How can we increase sales of a quality speciality product that qualified people want very much but basically can no longer afford to own? We'll look at some ways to get at the solution later. But first, let's take a little excursion.

Understanding the Mind

Before we go too far into techniques and processes for generating great ideas, it might be helpful to have an understanding of what we've got to work with. On the next few pages, we'll take a brief look at how the mind works. In this way we'll overcome barriers of which we may not have been aware.

Way 11 Understand why it's hard to generate ideas

It's hard work to generate ideas because we have never been taught how to do it. It's not part of our culture. When you were at school, did you learn about brain organisation? About thinking processes? About creativity? Not very likely.

So we grow up thinking that it's difficult to be an 'ideas person', they're born, not made, and we allow it to be so. We create barriers for ourselves based on this preconception, and we let them get in the way of the truth, which is that we *can*, in fact, generate great ideas.

It's tough because:
we think logically
we carry stereotypes in our minds
we are afraid to fail
we don't want to seem stupid
we don't want to be laughed at
we don't want to be thought odd.
Why is it so tough for you?

It's tough for me because:

_____

_____

_____

_____

_____

Way 12 Understand why it's easy to generate ideas

It's easy to generate ideas because we are inherently smart enough to learn the processes and techniques that enable us to do so. All it takes is a basic understanding, a little experience of the process, and the inhibitions will slip away.

When the inhibitions have gone, we get better at it.

Have you ever acted in a play? If so, you'll have noticed how difficult it is at first, and how it gets easier and easier as you keep rehearsing. The lines start to come. The moves seem to make sense. The timing begins to work. And eventually the autopilot takes over and it becomes very comfortable.

Have you ever watched an experienced piano player in a cocktail bar? Someone goes over and talks to him, and he carries on a conversation without missing a beat. All it takes is practice. An experienced touch typist can keep tapping away at the keyboard while chatting about the weather.

Or are you, as Lyndon Johnson used to say, one who 'can't walk and chew gum at the same time'.

What it takes is constant reiteration of various creative approaches, such as those in this book. Practise. Do it again. Build the experience. Your comfort level will rise. And you'll soon be generating great ideas for your own benefit.

Way 13 Understand right/left brain structure

The way I remember it is this. Left-handed people tend to be more artistic and creative than right-handers. The left side of the body is controlled by the right side of the brain. Thus the right side of the brain controls our creative, visual, spatial concepts. The left side of the brain controls our logical, mathematical, judgemental, analytical activities.

The point is that these are two different sets of functions, and the brain can be like a large steam engine. Once it gets moving in a direction, it tends to keep going. Let's prove it. Try this easy test:

What do you call a funny story? – *joke*
What are you when you have no money? – *broke*
What's another word for Coca Cola? – *Coke*
What's the white of an egg? —————

It isn't yolk, it's albumen. Were you tricked? Most people are. And that's what I mean. The brain likes to race ahead, because it already knows the answer.

If you keep bouncing back and forth between left-brain/right-brain activities, you'll get a headache. Thus the recommendation is to divide your time between the two types of activity. When you're dreaming up ideas, or mulling over problems, doodling on a pad, listening to music, that sort of thing, you are exercising your right brain. When you're sitting there saying, 'Now this would cost £12 per unit and we'd probably be able to pack 12 units in a case, so that would be £144 a case – so ten cases would be £1440. Ten cases is 120 units, and we can make 120 units for £100, so it looks like it would be profitable!' you're using your left brain.

That's why in a brainstorming session we suspend judgement while we're coming up with ideas. Evaluation and judgement get in the way of creativity. So we create, create, create. Then we switch over and evaluate, evaluate, evaluate, to arrive at the best conclusion.

Way 14 Avoid the logic trap

The mind wants things to work logically. We tend to organise everything into little compartments and keep it there. One word is all it takes to give you access to one of your compartments. Try it. Here are some words. What do they bring up in your mind? And what not?

- Holidays (sun, beach, hotels, rivers, scenery, airliners, trips?)
  (Not: a pile of bricks, a printing press, a violin?*)
- Rush hour (traffic jams, crowds, pushing, shoving, clocks?)
  (Not: a tiger in the jungle, a hang glider, a lake?**)
- Hospital (doctors, nurses, operations, medicine, needles?)
  (Not: a wedding, an operatic aria, a video camera?***)

*But if you spent a holiday learning to play the violin, it would be in that compartment.

**But if you commute to work by ferry across a lake, it would be in that compartment.

***But if you took your video camera to hospital to record the birth of your child, it would be in that compartment.

The logical structure of our compartments is so important that we tend to avoid something that is at variance with them. We want things to be orderly and 'right'. So when something intrudes into our logical patterns, we become uncomfortable – our comfort zone has been penetrated. We resist strange-seeming change. We expect things to happen logically, so we can anticipate the results of actions. If they don't happen logically, unexpected results can occur, and we can feel unhappy. So we avoid the unexpected by staying with the comfortable.

This is a barrier to generating great ideas. Some great ideas are seemingly illogical. We need to recognise this barrier and accept that it is there. We must give ourselves *permission* to act differently. It can be all right to be illogical. It is allowed. We must avoid the logic trap.

Way 15 Avoid the intelligence trap

Don't be fooled into thinking there's a logical link between highly intelligent people and highly creative people. The more intelligent a person is, the more they are likely to bring their vast experience (read preconceptions) to bear.

Do highly intelligent people have any natural claim to the appreciation of beauty? To a sense of humour? To style? To musical or artistic ability?

We tend to stereotype our images, one being of intelligence. Here are some job titles. Imagine you work at Central Casting, and you have to haul in some actors for the following roles. Who would they be?

- An airline captain (Concorde)
- An airline captain (Air Cubana)
- A biker (Harley Davidson variety)
- A New York City cop
- A London policeman (present day)
- A London bobby (turn of the century)
- A librarian
- The owner of a Pekingese
- A yuppie
- An inventor
- A computer nerd
- A Hollywood starlet
- A senior British Army officer (World War 2)
- A Vietnam era GI
- An African tribal warrior
- A French chef

- An Italian opera singer
- An old man in a pub

Got some good images? Picked some real actors? Now, I'm casting this film, and here are the people I've picked. Would they work for you?

- An airline captain (Concorde) — Danny de Vito
- An airline captain (Air Cubana) — Alec Guinness
- A biker (Harley Davidson variety) — Laurence Olivier
- A New York City cop — Terry Thomas
- A London policeman (present day) — Tom Cruise
- A London bobby (turn of the century) — Al Pacino
- A librarian — Kathleen Turner
- The owner of a Pekingese — Madonna
- A yuppie — George C Scott
- An inventor — Vanessa Redgrave
- A computer nerd — Harrison Ford
- A Hollywood starlet — Glenda Jackson
- A senior British Army officer (WW2) — John Candy
- A Vietnam era GI — James Mason
- An African tribal warrior — Harry Belafonte
- A French chef — John Mills
- An Italian opera singer — David Niven
- An old man in a pub — Chevy Chase

Now I'm sure these are (or were) all fine actors, but can you see them in these roles? Perhaps one or two, at a real stretch. In fact, it could probably be done (assuming they were still with us). But who would agree to it? Who would dare?

I can think of a couple of films where they got a bit daring and cast all kinds of big names in tiny little cameos – *It's A Mad, Mad, Mad, Mad World* and *Around The World in Eighty Days*. They both worked for me.

Tying yourself to stereotypes can be hazardous to your creativity, so don't get bogged down in the intelligence trap.

Way 16 Avoid the information trap

The more you know about a problem, the easier it is to solve. Oh yes? The problem is, we can be so close to the problem we get bogged down with information and ignore things we already know, so we don't consider them. 'Everybody knows that!' Fortunately, if you allow uninformed people to help you generate ideas, you may find the occasional solution popping up that is so clear, you want to kick yourself. 'Of course! It's so obvious!' (See Way 30.) So when you're trying to solve a problem, by all means involve people who know a lot about the subject. And include one or two who know nothing:

LADY BRACKNELL I have always been of the opinion that a man who desires to get married should know either everything or nothing. Which do you know?

JACK I know nothing, Lady Bracknell.

LADY BRACKNELL I am pleased to hear it. I do not approve of anything that tampers with natural ignorance. Ignorance is like a delicate exotic fruit; touch it and the bloom is gone.

The Importance of Being Earnest, Oscar Wilde

Way 17 Understand about your blah-blah-blah

All the time you're awake, there's this blah-blah-blah going on. Some people call it sub-vocalising, others call it sub-titles. It's this constant stream of judgements and comments that your subconscious releases. It's happening to you now, while you read this. Right?

Don't let it run you! It's there and there's nothing you can do about it, but too often it will tell you things that get in the way of a solution. You may have to make a conscious assertion to shut it up. Blah-blah-blah particularly gets in the way of your ability to listen. Something is said, and immediately you take off: 'Oh, that'll never work, not a hope, why don't they listen to me? These things never work and they want to spend all this money and the next thing you know they're out of business . . . speaking of money I must remember to stop at the cash machine on the way home tonight, I hope it's working, these things never work when you need them, the last time I really needed one I had to drive to three different places to get one that worked, and then I got a parking ticket! Damn! I forgot to pay that parking ticket, I bet it's expired and now I'll get a summons, I wonder where I put it, I really must tidy up my desk, I wonder what else I'll find'. Now, what were you saying?

Your blah-blah-blah will run you if you let it. You want it to keep as quiet as possible with the criticism and the judgements. Keep it in tune with your thinking. Let it be your partner rather than your opponent. 'That's good. You're doing well! I like it. We're coming along well. That could work. Try it, you'll like it. Ah, hah. Why not? Of course! Yes we can. We should. I will if you will'.

Building Your Own Creativity

This chapter is about opening your mind to possibilities. It gives you 13 approaches to building your own creativity, many of which you can use in your daily activities. Some of them are techniques, some are tools to take advantage of what comes up.

Everybody has creativity within themselves. Some people, who don't profess to be creative, can surprise themselves by being very much so when the right opportunities present themselves. There are many ways to put yourself in the position where these opportunities arise.

Let's make sure we're on common ground. My dictionary defines:

- *Creative* as: able to create; productive; inventive.

- *To create* as: to cause to come into existence; grow; bring into being; make; originate; bring about; give rise to.

- *Productive* as: producing abundantly; fertile.

- *To produce* as: bear; bring forth; yield.

- *Inventive* as: skilled or resourceful in inventing; indicating an ability to invent.

- *To invent* as: to come upon; meet with; discover; think up; devise or fabricate in the mind; think out or produce; originate; devise for the first time; find.

- *To discover* as: to find out; learn of the existence of; realise.

- *To devise* as: think out; contrive; plan; invent.

- *To think* as: to form or have in the mind; to conceive; determine; resolve; work out.

You can do all these things, can't you? Most of them? Some of them? That's what creativity is all about.

Way 18 Carry a pocket dictating machine

Have you noticed something about advancing age? The memory goes. Fortunately, technology is at hand in the shape of the pocket dictating machine. It's a notebook you talk into. I carry one always, and put it to work frequently to capture a thought or reminder I want to come back to. It might be a sign on a truck, the location of a shop spotted from a cab, or information from a story in the press.

I've built a database of advertising slogans and taglines – I call them slogos. I've turned this into a weekly contest that runs in *Marketing* magazine, called 'Name That Brand!' Everything that's in that database started out as a few words spoken into my machine. Sometimes, if I have a few minutes to spare, I'll go through some unfamiliar magazines in a library looking for new slogos, all recorded on the tiny cassette, to be input to my computer later.

Another use is at a trade exhibition. These crowded and bustling events are usually hard to assimilate. So walk around the exhibits and make verbal notes of interesting items. It's also a handy way to remember ideas that you get when you're driving. You may be stuck in a long traffic jam. Give yourself a brainstorming session on a project you're working on and get the thoughts on tape. If you have somehow left your little machine behind, and you need to record a note now, use the car phone, call your answering machine and leave a message on that!

Then every so often, rewind the tape, sit at your computer or with a notebook, and spew it all out. You'll be amazed at the little items you've recorded that you've since forgotten about. Hint: speak clearly. Pause for a second after you press the button before you talk, and wait a second after your message before you stop recording – otherwise you'll find yourself listening to bits of words at the beginning and end of each note – they tend to pile up on each other. Spell out strange words. It's very frustrating trying to work out what you said if you act carelessly.

Way 19 Use a computer idea outliner

I frequently use idea-outliner software on my Macintosh computer. An outliner lets you group and organise your thoughts into the best sequence. A good package is More, by Symantec. Some word-processing software has an outliner built in.

Here's how an outliner works: the software gives you the ability to create a series of headlines and subheads that relate at different levels with and between each other. By moving these about as you develop your ideas, you can quickly organise the thoughts into the right order for further work, such as writing a specification or a brief, or creating a proposal or presentation.

Let's say you were using an outliner to develop a book – this book, for example. When you start, you might list, in no particular order, a number of items you will address. You type each entry, and press the 'return' key after each one, producing a result like this:

- **Introduction**
- **Audiences**
- **Chapters**
- **Index**

Each of these items is a 'first-level headline'. All the items are of equal importance (at the same level), except they are in a certain sequence (which you can change, at will).

Now you want to start listing some chapter ideas, so you use the mouse (the computer's pointing-control device) to place the computer's pointer on the *Chapters* line and press the return key. This opens up a blank line beneath it. Using the mouse, you drag the entry to the right and it thus indents, so it looks like this:

+ **Chapters**
   - (NEXT LINE IS TYPED HERE)

This indentation means that the new entry line is a *sub-item* of the *Chapters* head. When this happens, the first-level head changes from – **Chapters** to + **Chapters,** the + sign indicating that there is a sub-item for this entry. Now you start typing in your ideas for chapters, pressing return after each one:

- **Introduction**
- **Audiences**
+ **Chapters**
   - Understanding problems
   - Understanding the mind
   - (NEXT LINE IS TYPED HERE)
- **Index**

As you make each new subhead entry under + **Chapters**, the next first-level head - *Index* slides down a line.

Now you are ready to start listing some of the ideas within each chapter. Let's say you decide to start with the chapter on *Understanding problems*. You want to develop a series of ideas relevant to that section. So you use the mouse to move the pointer to that line and press the return key. You get this:

- **Introduction**
- **Audiences**
+ **Chapters**
   - Understanding problems
   - (NEXT LINE IS TYPED HERE)
   - Understanding the mind

- Building your own creativity
- Generating ideas in groups
- Techniques to develop solutions
- Techniques to measure ideas
- **Index**

You then use the mouse to drag the entry point to the right, and start inputting the ideas for this category:

+ **Chapters**
    + Understanding problems
        - Define the current situation
        - Define the goal, and make it measurable
        - Identify the gaps
        - Identify the core problem you are trying to solve
        - (NEXT LINE IS TYPED HERE)
    - Understanding the mind
    - Building your own creativity

Now comes the nifty part about the outliner. It's the ability to hide information you are not currently using, so that it doesn't get in the way when you're working on something else. And this concealment is as temporary as you want it to be. With a couple of deft moves of the mouse, you can collapse all the entries to the first-level heads or you can go into any section you're interested in and display *its* subheads. All at the click of a mouse. You can collapse it back again just a bit:

+ **Chapters**
    + Understanding problems
    - Understanding the mind
    - Building your own creativity
    - Generating ideas in groups

Or you can collapse it further:

- **Introduction**
- **Audiences**

+ **Chapters**
- **Index**

By not bogging you down with vast amounts of extraneous detail all the time, the outliner lets you work on the big picture, then the little picture, then another part of the picture, just as you wish. You can move whole chunks of information with ease, and in this way, you can simply build the logic of the end product.

When you've finished with the outlining step, you can quickly transfer the text you've created into a word-processing program and start creating the final document. Some outliners are so sophisticated, they let you create slides, overhead transparencies or an on-screen presentation, after you've built your outline. It takes just a few key strokes to do this, and then you can keep your people informed, or make the presentation to the client, or whatever.

I have often used a computer outliner as the basis for a brainstorming session when there are only maybe two or three people participating. The beauty of this is that when the session is finished, it's all there in the computer, ready to be manipulated into a document. Otherwise, you've got all these notes on flip-chart sheets. Then what do you do? The outliner helps to solve that problem.

Way 20 Give your senses a workout

All your senses can help you build your creativity. But you have to keep them active. Your senses of sight, hearing, smell, taste and touch get various inputs through the day, but it doesn't take long to acclimatise yourself to a new sensation and tune it out.

- When you first walk into a cow shed or pig farm, you'll notice an overwhelming stench that could make you retch. But spend a few minutes there and you won't notice it.

- Enter a motorway and you see how fast all the cars are going (assuming you haven't come to an instant traffic jam!). You accelerate and keep up with them. You drive at 70 mph for a while, then slow to 40 mph and you think you're crawling along.
- Come into the house from a cold evening and it may seem stifling with the heat on, and you stand there complaining of the sauna-like atmosphere, while the occupants of the room scream at you to close the door because of the cold draught.

Notice how sensory inputs can bring up memories? The smell of turkey cooking makes you think of Christmas, a certain song reminds you of a romantic evening long ago. The feel of velvet makes you think of a certain chair or room.

Here's an exercise you can do when you're able to close your eyes for a while and fantasise. Pick a familiar object, then go through the five senses with it in your imagination. Take a banana. As you complete each sense, bring up a memory that is suggested. If your memory takes you on a trip, go along for the ride, then try and return and carry on. You may be amazed.

- *Sight*. Think of its appearance. Imagine the colour and the slight bruises. Is it part of a bunch? How is the stalk? How ripe is it? What does the flesh look like? What about the cross-section when you slice it? What about the dimensions? Is there a brand label or price sticker on the outside?
- *Hearing*. Think of what the peel sounds like coming off, what it sounds like when you bite into it, when you eat it with a spoon, the sound someone would make if they stepped on the skin hurriedly.
- *Smell*. Imagine the subtle odour. Do you like it? How about a perfume made of this essence? Create the smell of a banana milk shake.

- *Taste.* Savour the flavour. I remember Punch and Judy children's toothpaste when I was young, with banana flavour being a favourite.
- *Touch.* Notice in your mind the smooth texture of the skin, the squishy feel of an overripe fruit, the weight, the feeling of the peeled banana in your fingers, in your mouth.

You don't *have* to use a banana. Try it with something else. When you're working to solve a problem, evaluate the problem in the same way. What does it look like? What does it sound like? What does it smell, taste, feel like? What do these sensations suggest? It's all right if the problem is an abstraction. Apply your senses to it anyway, and see what comes up.

Way 21 Study something familiar for ten minutes

To prove why you should do this, start by drawing something you know well from memory, such as the face of your watch, the front of your house, the dashboard of your car, the inside of your kitchen.

No doubt you'll find the rendering a trifle inaccurate when you compare it with reality.

We tend to take familiar things for granted and retain only a cursory image in our minds. The task here is to exercise your perceptive skills. So take something you're familiar with, and spend about ten minutes studying it. A daffodil, a strawberry, your engagement ring, your cat's face. Suppose you had to describe it to a police artist. Close your eyes and visualise it. Then take a piece of paper and draw it. How close did you get?

Building your creativity means sharpening your mind, and that means heightening your perceptions.

Don't stop with visualisation. Listen to your favourite piece of music. Can you sing every note along with it? Can you predict what the next note is going to be when you play it? Can you go through it after you've finished playing it? Start playing it, sing along with it, turn the volume down, but keep singing (it's all right, you can do it just to yourself). After a minute or two, turn the volume up and see if you're in the same place.

Take a tomato. Feel the skin as you bite into it. Take a bit and put it on different parts of your tongue. One part of your tongue is sensitive to sweetness, another to tartness. Can you detect where? Savour the tomato as you eat it. Sniff a honeysuckle. Mmm. Sniff an open jar of fish paste. Mmm? Close your eyes, turn out the lights and feel your way around your living room at night.

When you think you've heightened your senses, take a walk on a crowded hard pavement and *listen*. Do the people's footsteps seem louder? They do for me. These are all ways of enhancing your sensitivities. And that will help your mind work more actively.

Way 22 Don't wait until the day before the deadline to start thinking about a problem

One of the amazing things about ideas is that you can let your brain work on autopilot. If you give it the basic concepts and a variety of relevant stimuli, eventually it will come back with concepts for you to work on. Now there is a terrible tendency, when faced with a problem, to leave it all until the last minute. 'I always work best under pressure!' That's the usual line, isn't it? And it's true. The pressure of a deadline concentrates the mind wonderfully.

However, you're not giving your brain a fair crack at it. If you have to produce something in two weeks, and you'd normally start on it a day or two before it's due, try starting on it right away. Not to take it to fruition, but just to give yourself enough input to be aware of the dimensions of the situation.

So read the brief. Read the background articles. Look at the video. Talk to a couple of people. Then carry on as before. Your thinking will continue subconsciously, as you go about your other activities. The raw facts that you reviewed can go on the back burner and simmer away for a while, soaking up the marinade of your experience. All you have to do is stir the pot once in a while, to make sure the ingredients don't stick. Then, when you're ready, you can get down to it with the benefit of some serious subterranean thinking having been at work. Try it.

Way 23 Close your eyes and let your mind wander

Daydreaming works wonders, when you're not driving or working heavy machinery. InterCity are onto a good thing in their advertising about what can happen to you while taking a train journey. There's nothing better than to be sitting back in a fully reclined seat on an airliner, having a cognac, eyes closed, listening to the music through the stereo headphones. Every so often, you can look out of the window at the cloud formations, or better still, a sunset. If you hit it right, you can watch a sunset for an hour or more when you're flying westbound.

Letting your subconscious work on a problem in this kind of environment can be very effective. Try setting yourself up by laying out the facts before you go into reverie mode. Look at some of the documentation first. Review in your mind where you are now, where you want to be, and what's in the way of getting there. Have your pocket recorder or notebook handy. You may need it.

Way 24 Sleep on it

It's impossible to switch your brain off. It just keeps on churning away. Sometimes it does what you want it to. And sometimes it does what it wants to. Take advantage of this. Especially when sleeping. You can go to bed with a variety of problems scrambling around in your mind, doze off, and in the morning, find a realistic solution waiting for you. Be proactive about it. Before you shut down, review the situation as clearly as you can in your mind. Talk to yourself. State the identified problem. State the present position and the desired position. State any barriers you want to overcome. Then say 'It's all yours.'

I find it hard to sleep sometimes when I'm loaded down with a problem-solving assignment. In this case I've found it helpful to sleep with my Walkman on, playing relaxing music. You can also get self-hypnosis tapes on subjects like creativity that can be quite fun to use.

Always have notebook and pen or your pocket tape machine handy to record what comes up the moment you get it. Or you'll forget it. I had a vivid dream recently that completely laid out an internal communications programme I needed. It ended up as a 20-page document. Now all we've got to do is sell it!

Way 25 Break your travel routine

How do you normally take a regular journey? Do you vary it much, if at all? Do every journey as a tourist would, agog at what you see. Look in the windows of strange little shops. Keep your mind open and let it 'go with the flow'. Drop in and look around. See what types of people are in there. Imagine a current problem you're trying to solve being related to what or whom you see as you meander. How would *this* connect with *that*?

Way 26 Break your reading routine

I love picking up a discarded newspaper or magazine on the train. With any luck it'll be an unfamiliar publication. Trade magazines are especially interesting. The first time I picked up a copy of a magazine aimed at undertakers (sorry, morticians – this was in the USA), what amazed me were the ads for hearses. They were full colour double-page spreads, and they showed grinning 'young couple' role models standing by their death chariots, as if they were the coolest of convertibles.

If you don't pick up other people's leavings, or the idea offends you, go to the library, or ask for something different when the flight attendant offers you reading matter on a trip. Or buy something different at the news-stand.

Reading the advertising, especially the small ads that would only be placed in this publication to appeal to its limited, specialised, audience, is fascinating. Also look at the short bits in the overview sections near the front. There's all kinds of interesting stuff going on.

Once again, read with some existing idea or problem in the back of your mind. Seek out opportunities to make a connection between what you come across and what you're working on.

Read actively, too. Use a highlighter to stress interest-ing thoughts. Clip articles out of the paper. Record a point on your pocket cassette machine. Make a note in your Filofax.

Way 27 Break your television and radio routine

When you really feel like some good solid punishment, spend an evening watching TV, but never shows that you would normally watch. As with all this break-up-your-routine routine, we want to shake you out of your rut. Never watch TV in the morning? Try it one am. Never watch TV at 3 am? You'll be amazed at what's on. How about some game shows? With an Astra satellite dish, you can receive the JSTV channel. This is two hours a day of real Japanese television – news, game shows, drama, documentaries. Absolutely fascinating. I also watch the news in German, a language I don't speak, but want to learn. And there's Dutch and French program-ming, too. French TV newscasts use a wider frame for the newscaster than do British or American, to fit their hands into the picture, since they use them more in telling the story.

The same suggestions apply to radio, of course. Have you ever listened to the phone-in shows in the middle of the night?

Way 28 Break your food routine

Go to a strange restaurant. Ask for guidance on what to order. Or go to a familiar restaurant and order something totally different from your usual. Buy a new exotic cookbook and try out some new recipes. Shake yourself out of your food/tastes rut.

Some ethnic restaurants have good explanations of their dishes on the menu. Read them and try. Note preferences on your portable tape machine (see Way 18).

Look at what other people are having at nearby tables and ask the server what it is.

Way 29 Browse in a bookshop or library

Whenever I have to meet someone in town and there is a chance I may have to wait, I arrange to meet in a bookshop. That way I can keep occupied until they show up. As an author, I like to see what's hot, and what's not (ie, what's on the remainder tables).

It's interesting to go into a shop or library trying to become informed on a new subject. That's one of the advantages of being a freelance writer – you never know what you're going to be asked to write about next, and suddenly you have to become knowledgeable on a strange subject very fast. You can even get ideas for books that don't exist. You go in cold, looking for information about a subject. First you look for it yourself, going to the most logical place. If you don't find what you're looking for, then ask at the desk. This is where it gets interesting. The way you have the subject cate-gorised may be quite different from the way they have.

Take aviation books. In some shops they're grouped under 'Sports' *(Learning to Fly)*, in others under 'Military' *(The Fabulous Spitfire)*, in others under 'Transport' *(Civil Airliners of the 80s)*. Some even have them under 'Aviation'. The interesting thing about these variations is that you find yourself unexpectedly looking at books on scuba diving, the Battle of Trafalgar and great steam engines of the GWR. Pick one of those up and look through it. Hmm. Other shops group them by publisher. 'Penguin books are *here*. Kogan Page books are *there*.'

When you're doing this browsing, keep looking for *connections* to your current project or problem. How would *this* affect *that?* Suppose we had a book that did *this?*

Way 30 Open your eyes and look at the architecture

Next time you go into an old building – a major edifice in an older part of town – take a look at the design features. Look at the ceiling, at the entrance, at the facade. It is quite amazing what details abound that you'd normally never notice. Too often we seem to carry around a glaze that we spray on everything we come into contact with so that we just get the superficial overview. What we should do is open our eyes and see what's before us! Put yourself in the shoes of the architect or the builder. How did they accomplish that feature? Why is that turret there? How would the traffic be if the building was turned around 180 degrees?

There was this big new building, a skyscraper, with many lifts. The trouble was the lifts were too slow, so people were spending much too long waiting. There were lots of complaints, from tenants and visitors alike. Something had to be done. It would have cost millions to take the lifts out and install faster ones, to say nothing of major disruption of an important and busy new building. The problem was solved after a suggestion from the hall porter, for only a few thousand. What do you think they did? (See page 58 for the answer.)

On many older buildings you'll see gargoyles or little statues, usually well above ground level. Toronto's Old City Hall has a set of gargoyles of fantastic medieval characters, and suddenly there's this modern-looking man at the end there who happens to have been the architect – doing a sort of Alfred Hitchcock personal appearance in his own work.

All this gazing is to help stimulate your thoughts by changing your normal attitude to a city. Let your imagination be prompted by what you see. Ideas will arise that will amaze you.

Way 31 Visit a usual department store or shopping mall – unusually

We become conditioned so fast that it's easy to walk around a familiar shopping location on autopilot. We're looking for one or two specific items and we know where they are. We reach for the item and leave. What I'm suggesting is that you walk round a familiar shopping centre with open eyes. Look for something you don't normally want. Go into the speciality boutiques. See how the displays are set out. Imagine you were the producer of one of the products on display. How would you improve the way it's being shown? Look for interesting signs and 'dressing'. Stimulate your creative juices by imagining a challenge – how would you deal with *this* corner? Suppose *those* goods had to be sold by tonight, what would you do?

Look at the cash desks or checkout locations. Here's where the impulse items are placed. Do a survey of impulse items, and see what conclusions you can draw about fads and fashions. Look at the window displays. These are often the most creative elements of a store, and may give you some ideas. What three things would you change to make things better for sales? For the customer?

Hardware or do-it-yourself stores and stationery stores are fascinating. Browsing through these can produce all kinds of inputs to the mind for subsequent sifting and allocation. Another type of shop that's interesting is the gift shop, especially those that sell limited-edition crafts. There may be one place in the world where these items are sold, and you are there. What's being made in our cottages? What is the message from the outback?

Way 32 Visit unusual shops

Browsing through strange shopping areas is fascinating. Places like a ship's chandler, a sporting-equipment store or a car-parts store may be unfamiliar territory to you. Or a street market you haven't been to before, or one of those antique shopping markets where there are lots of little boutiques, but in a strange town. The flea markets in Paris – le Marché aux Puces de St Ouen – are well worth a visit.

Go to such places with a problem you're trying to solve. Walk around, looking for solutions suggested by what you see. Try to relate what you want to achieve to the strange artifacts you find at every turn. When you're in a foreign country, visit supermarkets and hardware stores to see the differences in products, gadgetry and marketing approaches.

Way 33 Visit an art gallery or museum, and take a child

When did you last visit a major art gallery or museum? If your answer is 'none of the above' hie yourself to one, and take a young person along with you.

There will often be special children's projects to perform, that you can pick up at the front desk. If you have these, it makes the visit more involving and interactive. So as well as helping the kids build their creativity, maybe you can get some inputs to your own. Maybe you can create some personal involvement (you have to be fairly old to do this). The Imperial War Museum Aviation Collection at Duxford in Cambridgeshire has a huge collection of aircraft, and on display is a Miles Magister aeroplane, G-AFBS. This happens to be the *actual aircraft* in which I took my very first flying lesson, at Denham Aerodrome, when I was 15 years old!

Way 34 Visit a trade show or exhibition

Just about every special interest has some kind of trade show or exhibition, and there are plenty of shows that cross borders, covering a variety of interests.

If you want to see the state of the art in your area of interest, these are the places to go. And if you want a fast immersion in an area with which you're not very familiar, exhibitions are also great. Aim to go on the trade days – avoid the public days. Don't worry if you're not in the industry. If you have a business card, you can usually pass the registration needs at the front desk. If nothing else, you're there because you want to know more about the business, pending an investment.

If you're really interested in something you see at a particular exhibit, try to hook up with the chief person at the stand and have a chat. The smiling hostesses anxious to pin a badge on your lapel won't tell you much.

Go with an open mind, and be willing to take the occasional brochure for later review. Take plenty of business cards. Walk around with the objective of looking for ideas. You'll see all kinds of innovative displays, use of interactive techniques, demonstration styles, gadgets and devices. At last year's Farnborough Air Show I saw an audio-visual technique at the Lockheed Aircraft stand that blew my mind, incorporating a miniature videotaped presenter walking around a full-sized instrument panel from a Hercules aircraft. Quite incredible. How are videowalls being used? Look at how live action is integrated with video. Look for break-throughs in holography. Look for computer displays. What sorts of giveaway are being offered? Seek out new ways of telling stories. Is anyone using actors to put on a little play? Watch it. You'll see a lot that's fresh at a trade show. (And a lot that's not.)

Way 35 Watch a familiar film

Thanks to video machines we can plug into a favourite film as many times as we want. I must have seen *Star Wars* over 100 times. And *An American In Paris*. The activity proposed here involves rewatching the movie, but now putting yourself in the shoes of one of the crew members. Be the director. Look at how the shots are framed. Look at how the camera moves. Relish really beautiful sequences and play them again and again. A favourite is the sequence in Alfred Hitchcock's *Frenzy* that starts at the top of the stairs and backs down them slowly and smoothly, starting in silence, with the sounds of the street gradually building – as we eventually pull back right outside – all in one long, continuous move. How did they do that?

Delight in obvious howlers – the exterior shot of the castle in the medieval story *Ivanhoe*, with a red double decker bus going by in the background. The little screw tumbling out of the cockpit canopy in a close-up in *Sound Barrier*, when the pilot is being shaken as he approaches the speed of sound at 40,000 feet. Or go for continuity. Look for jumps – a different hairdo from one scene to the next, a glass not full and then full in two adjacent shots. Hands on hips cutting to arms folded. Noticing these little lapses helps to build your awareness.

Look at the supporting actors in group scenes. Follow one background person and see how they behave during the foreground action. Watch how the extras work. Put yourself in their place for a moment. During a dance sequence, follow the third chorus girl from the right, rather than the star in the centre.

Way 36 Don't say 'But', say 'And'

Have you noticed how we use the word 'but' all the time? 'I'd love to go to the beach today, *but* I have to work.' 'I'd love to help, *but* I'm busy right now.' 'I'd love to go out with you *but* I'm washing my hair tonight.' 'I like it, *but* . . . ' What a bunch of turn-offs!

But means except, with the exception of; save; otherwise than; other than; yet; still.

Now take those same statements and use 'and' instead of 'but'. 'I'd love to go to the beach today, *and* I have to work.' Maybe you can do both? 'I'd love to help, *and* I'm busy right now.' So help when you've finished! 'I'd love to go out with you *and* I'm washing my hair tonight.' So why not come and assist! 'I like it, *and* . . . '

And means also; in addition; moreover; as well as. Try forcing yourself to say *and* when you're about to say *but* and see what happens. You may be amazed! Barriers will fall, because they are not there when you banish the *but*. But make sure you do it, no, no, *and* make sure you do it!

Way 37 Take another's point of view

This is based on *if*. *If* you were your customer, how would you seem to him or her? *If* you were the journalist you're having lunch with, what would he or she think of you? *If* you were the salesperson, how would you react to the pitch you're expected to make? *If* you were the judge hearing your plea, what would you think of your case? *If* you were the viewer watching your commercial, what would you think? Would you get the message?

People bring their own unique perceptions to bear on everything they do. They translate everything they relate to into their own terms. Thus if you speak *your* language to them, will they understand? What is *their* language? Contrast the types of stories and writing style in a tabloid newspaper with those of a quality daily. Take a look at the same story, and see how it's treated by *The Sun* and *The Times*. Or the *New York Post* and *The New York Times*. Then look at the typical readers of these papers. How would a *Times* reader react to a tabloid treatment of a serious story? How would a *Sun* reader react to a *Times* report on, say, the Budget?

Suppose you were trying to generate a media story about your latest venture. How would your targeted magazine editor react to your proposal? The answer is, 'What's in it for me? What's in it for my readers? Why should I take my valuable space and write about your puny activities?' To sell your story successfully, you would have to bring out the benefits of running it to the editor. You may have to appeal to any of a variety of emotions – fear, greed, spite, compassion, a sense of the ridiculous, what else?

Ask yourself: 'How do I want this person to react to this idea?' Then identify what it would take to get that reaction. Step into their moccasins and look at the idea. Note your reactions. Then act accordingly.

Way 38 Play squiggles

My mother used to play this with me when we sat in the air-raid shelter during World War 2. I've been playing it with kids ever since. All you need is some paper and a pen or pencil. You do a squiggle on the page and hand it over. The partner has to turn the squiggle into a picture of something. They quickly discover they're allowed to turn the page around and look at it from different points of view. It helps to have a time deadline.

Squiggle   *Result*

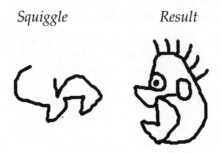

You'll often be surprised at the results. You may try to ordain an idea, but... I once gave my oldest daughter, Stephanie, what was quite obviously a staircase to develop. She turned it into a dinosaur.

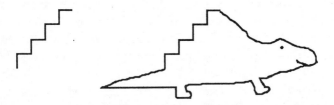

Way 39 Play 'What else could this be?'

This is another favourite game I've often played with my children in their early years. The idea is to show the child an ordinary household object, such as a saucepan or a corkscrew, and ask them 'What else could this be?' I'd show the kid two or three examples of what I meant, and then let them carry on. As time went by, we'd play it at any time, on a long train or plane trip, or while waiting for service in a restaurant. Very soon, the child picks up on the concept and needs no prompting. As they grow older, they take over and initiate the game themselves. What's amazing is the veritable gush of ideas that flows out – almost faster than the child can speak. The translation into real life is that the child becomes an effective lateral thinker, not bogged down by artificial constraints. And so will you.

Way 40 Listen to what the rules don't say

My chief guru, Geoff Nightingale of SynerGenics, often uses this illustration when he's starting up an interactive idea-development session with a group of people. It's the nine-dot exercise – usually found in the back pages of in-flight magazines, along with the crossword puzzles and duty-free listings.

The task is to draw four straight lines that will go through all the dots without raising pencil from paper. You can start anywhere, and end anywhere, but each new line must be connected with its predecessor. Go ahead. You have three minutes. See page 59 for the answer.

Or try this one. You have six matchsticks of identical length. Make four triangles with them.

Go ahead. You have three minutes. See page 59 for the answer.

Way 41 Think laterally

The ability to make apparently non-logical connections is the idea behind lateral thinking.

Edward de Bono, the lateral thinking expert, describes it this way: vertical thinking – beginning with one concept and then continuing with that concept until a solution is reached – is like digging one hole deeper and deeper; lateral thinking – exploring alternative ways to look at a problem before evolving a solution – is like digging lots of holes in different places.

How do you suppose they find oil? Drilling a hole deeper and deeper won't help you find oil if there's none there. But drilling lots of holes in the general area of suspicion will give you a much better chance at hitting a gusher.

Looking for oil – who has the best chance of success?

vertical   **lateral**

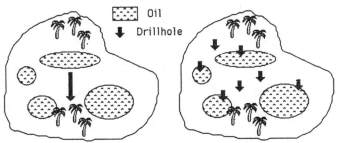

How can you organise yourself to think laterally? If you have been practising many of the exercises in this chapter you will be going in the right direction.

To get involved in solving your problem, make a conscious effort to think laterally.

Answer to Way 30: Open your eyes and look at the architecture

This is about identifying the *real* problem. It wasn't that the lifts were too slow, it was that people became irritated and bored waiting for them. The suggestion was to install mirrors in the lobbies, so people could study their favourite subject while waiting. It worked!

Answer to Way 40: Listen to what the rules don't say

The task is to draw four straight lines that will go through all the dots without raising pencil from paper. You can start anywhere, and end anywhere, but each new line must be connected with its predecessor. Nobody said anything about staying in the box! If you had trouble with this it's probably because you gave yourself a rule that didn't exist – to stay within the box. You are, in fact, allowed to step out of the box, and that is what to do with your thinking.

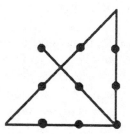

The triangles? Make a pyramid! Nobody said you had to think in two dimensions:

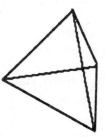

So this way is to *step out of the box!*

Generating Ideas in Groups

Gathering groups of people together to develop ideas is an effective approach, if handled properly. It can also be a waste of everyone's time if you get the technique wrong. The dynamics of a think-tank or brainstorming session are different from those of other meetings. The situation appears to be less formal, and the participants may be people who are not used to working with each other.

There are protocols that need to be observed, ranging from how the meeting is run and what may not be said, to how the people should sit. So what seems to be an informal process has a lot of hidden formality to it.

On the next few pages are 17 ways to make the task of generating ideas in groups more effective.

Way 42 Have a brainstorming session

A brainstorming session, or think-tank, helps you to generate a lot of ideas quickly. It is based on the premise that a group of people working together, under good direction, can evolve a wider variety of ideas and possibilities than those same people working as individuals. Brainstorming sessions can be a lot of fun.

The advantages of brainstorming come from there being a lower level of inhibition within the group compared with a more formal meeting, and a higher level of enthusiasm. Individual competitiveness needs to be managed so that it doesn't create barriers caused by one person trying to top another all the time.

Don't have too many people in the session (a maximum of eight, plus the facilitator and maybe a scribe, is a good guideline). Don't run it for too short a time (you need at least three to four hours to do a good job).

Way 43 Create a briefing memo

It's helpful for the participants to receive a briefing document one or two days before a brainstorming session. This should contain the following information:

- Location, date, time (start and finish)
- Subject (brand, client, product, service, etc)
- A definition of the end product required, for example:
  - Identification of problem to be solved
  - A new strategy
  - A series of ideas from an existing strategy
  - Story ideas for a campaign
  - Event ideas to generate publicity
  - New product-distribution methods
  - Name ideas for a new product or service
  - What to do with a redundant resource
  - Ways to improve quality
  - How to deal with new competitive activity, etc
- Deadline needs of the end product
- Who is participating in the session and any special requirements of individuals named
- Supporting background material (and not too much).

Way 44 Use a facilitator

Brainstorming sessions require an experienced facilitator to direct and control the meeting. The facilitator's role is *not* to make up ideas, but to assist the participants in evolving them.

Look at what happens otherwise. People often come to meetings with a hidden agenda. It may very well have something to do with looking good, or with not looking bad. Thus if they manage to score, according to their agenda, by evolving the ultimate idea, they have *won*. Or if they managed to lie low and not get found out as the incompetent they secretly know themselves to be, they have also won. If they came to the last meeting to win, and were beaten by a colleague, it might now be on their personal agenda somehow to defeat the colleague this time around. So if they manage to vanquish the colleague this time, they have won. And so on.

Too often people attend a meeting and listen to others only to find out when there's a momentary enough lull for them to inject their input to the conversation. They're not absorbing any information, they're waiting for the noise to stop, so they can start their own version. Have you noticed how people who think they're big shots – whom I call the *highest common dominator* – often use long verbal pauses between words to maintain the noise level in their corner, and cut down on interruptions? Like this:

'Well, *aaah* we've been looking at this for a long time *aaah* so we're very keen to have some *aaah* results that will let us *aaah* come to a decision *aaah* and another thing *aaah* blah blah blah.' Fortunately they have to breathe at some point, giving their competitor a chance to cut in.

But a brainstorming session isn't about the people in the room winning private little battles. It's about agreeing and solving a problem. So the role of the facilitator is to direct the group on to an effective path towards doing that. The facilitator needs to concentrate on evolving and identifying possibilities.

The skills that a facilitator must possess include:

- Ability to stand in front of a group of people and communicate about the task intelligently and interestingly
- Ability to present a high energy level, to detect the group's energy level, and to raise it if it wanes
- Ability to recognise and deal with emerging traits among the participants

- Meeting dominators
- Shrinking violets

- Ability to direct the proceedings along lines that will produce results, and to detect when the group is getting off track

- Ability to subjugate personal ideas in favour of the group's input

- Awareness of various techniques for developing ideas from groups

- Good sense of timing

- Ability to recognise opportunities that arise that may not be clearly articulated in the first instance.

Way 45 Plan the session

The facilitator should plan the session out beforehand. Look at the total time available and allocate blocks to specific areas. A four-hour session might look like this:

Item	Time allocation Hours Minutes		Time remaining Hours Minutes	
State purpose of session, define problem, obtain agreement to task		30	3	30
Identify strategic concepts that address problem		45	2	45
Evaluate strategies		15	2	30
Pick core strategy and define		15	2	15
Identify ideas that flow out of strategy		45	1	30
Evaluate ideas		15	1	15
Work out selected ideas	1	00		15
Summarise results, allocate tasks		15		00

Even if the plan is not as formally structured as this, the facilitator should have a good idea of timing constraints and allocate the time resource efficiently. Flexibility is the keynote, however. If you're on a roll, don't stop! Run into overtime if necessary.

Way 46 Use a non-threatening room layout

The layout should be open, with all the people facing each other.

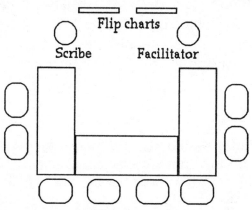

They should all be able to see what the facilitator and scribe are doing. There should be a way to hang the flipchart sheets on the walls around the room as they are removed from the pads. In the centre, between the tables, you might want to have a small table with examples of the product or whatever it is you're discussing, on hand.

Way 47 Abandon negative reactions

When you want to put your group into idea-developing mode, you should abandon the constraints that you normally live with. Don't allow any negative thoughts to surface. Don't allow people to step on or kill other people's 'babies'. 'Oh, that'll never work. It'll be much too expensive, and besides, we'd never get approval in time.' 'That's crazy. Who would want a thing like that?' or the insidious 'I know that this is a brainstorming session and we're not allowed to make negative comments, and I really like the idea, but . . . ' These sorts of comment serve to set up opponents within the room. A person who has been stepped on will either retreat and say no more, negating his or her existence in the meeting, or, worse, will become aggressive and look for opportunities to hit back. Petty warfare you don't need.

I sometimes use a 'fines box' when I run brainstorming sessions. Anyone uttering a negative is required to deposit a predetermined sum in the charity collection box on the table, and a big deal is made by all. If it worked and you earned no donations, you can appeal to the group's conscience by saying, at the end of the session: 'That was great! No negatives, and nothing for Save the Children. Did anyone have any negative *thoughts* they want to expiate (rattle rattle)?'

A good way to deal with an idea that is clearly negative to all is to say something like, 'Hmm. How can we make this work? Does this lead to any other way of solving the problem?'

The point is, there is a difference in the way our brains work between idea-developing mode and idea-evaluating mode (see Way 13). When you're developing ideas, your goal is lots of ideas, not lots of *great* ideas. You can do the weeding later. If you keep bouncing back and forth between creating and judging, you'll become inhibited and the ideas won't flow smoothly.

Way 48 Write it down before you lose it

The facilitator, or a designated scribe, should write everything down that comes up in a brainstorming session. This serves two purposes. One, it makes sure that nothing is missed. Two, it shows everyone that anything they say may be taken down and used against them. But seriously, it shows that no idea is too stupid or useless to avoid recording for possible future consideration.

In the best of all possible worlds, in addition to a scribe working at flipcharts, I'll have a person sitting at a computer taking everything down on an idea outliner (see Way 19) so that we can save time when we're ready to convert the session into a document.

The same rule applies as the session goes on. People tend to interrupt each other and start their own little trends. You're hot on the trail of an idea about curbing drink driving, and two or three people are oozing with great stuff, hitting off each other, growing and developing some exciting concept. Vanessa is holding forth, and is on a run. In the corner is Harry, who's been saying nothing for a few minutes. Suddenly, and without warning, Harry sits up. 'Umbrellas!' he shouts, triumphantly, interrupting Vanessa, who glares at him. His remark intrudes and takes Vanessa off the subject. 'Write it down, Harry! We'll get to it in a moment.' If you have a chance, write the word on the flip chart so you can come back to it. Then, when Vanessa has had her say, it's 'Now, Harry, what's this about umbrellas?'

Way 49 Encourage participation

It's very important when you're brainstorming that everybody joins in. You don't want observers. Some people naturally want to take over the meeting, while others want to retreat into their shell and make just the occasional fleeting comment, and then only when asked. It's the job of the facilitator to make sure that all the people are involved. If it is seen that one person is lying low, they should be encouraged to contribute. And meeting hogs should also be controlled without deflating their egos too much. The facilitator must remain in command all the time.

Here are some lines that might be helpful in handling the group:

Situation	Line
Opening up a shrinking violet	'Terry, what do you think? How would this work for you?'
Shutting down a dominator (James)	'Good, James, I think we've got that. Gillian, how'd you expand on this concept?'
Encouraging a contributor	'Yes, great! And what else?'
Getting a contributor to clarify	'We've got to write this down. What are the words we should use?'
	'Let me see if I understand you. What you mean is . . . '
	'You're going a little too fast. I have to capture this. Is it this . . . ?'
Handling someone's negative reaction	'If there was a way to make this work, would this be a solution for our list? Can we turn it around?'
	'It's really interesting though. What do we have to do to make it work?'
Dealing with an interrupter who has a different idea	'I just want to handle one thing at a time. Can you write it down and we'll get back to it? Don't lose it!'
Handling a seemingly foolish suggestion	'Good! See? Any idea is allowed. Let me write that down.'
Looking for input from others	'What do you get when you hear that? Jane? Tom?'

Way 50 Make a clay model of the problem

This is a good technique to employ near the beginning of a session, because it demonstrates that everyone can be creative, it involves all the people right away, and it breaks the ice. Ask them to make a three-dimensional model of the problem, or the brand, or the service, whatever. It springs people away from their preconceptions and prejudices. It also warms up the participants in anticipation of the work to be done. It shows that this meeting is going to be different, and fun.

I recently held a brainstorming session in a client's executive dining-room. So I got hold of a large serving platter and laid out strips of Plasticine as if they were canapés. Then, at the right moment, I became a waiter and served each participant with their choice of colours. Next, I asked them to make a model of their latest product (a training film).

The results were beautiful. All different, all demonstrating varying perceptions of what the film would do. They had five minutes to make their models, and then each person was asked to describe their creation and what it meant. The collection of little models can later be put on display as a conversation piece in someone's office.

Way 51 Outlaw side conversations

Sometimes during a brainstorming session you'll find little side meetings developing, with two or three centres of conversation going on simultaneously. They must be stopped. 'Just one meeting, please!' is the cry. 'If you've got something to contribute, let's all hear about it. It may even solve the problem!'

Way 52 Get people from different disciplines

A fresh point of view is always valuable. Don't just have the people who work on the problem in a brainstorming session. The group should ideally be made up of one or two specialists, one or two generalists, perhaps the client, and one or two outsiders to the problem. You don't really want much more than eight people.

Way 53 Adopt a questioning attitude

When we are young, the way we find out about things is to ask questions. The trouble is, this trait is progressively educated out of us as adults become increasingly fed up with explaining everything in sight. As we get older, there is more and more tendency to accept what we're told. This unfortunately leads to a major inhibition to the evolution of great ideas. Because the more we accept the situation that exists without challenging it, the less need or reason there is to change or innovate.

Way 54 Go for quantity, not quality

Our brains work differently when we are creating from when we are evaluating. So a large part of the group session should be devoted to developing lots of ideas, without worrying whether they are good or bad, expensive or cheap, manageable or not. The issue is not 'Will it work?' but 'Can we come up with any more?'

Way 55 Learn to listen

Why do we have so much difficulty listening to other people? Is it because other people are basically boring and have little of any interest to tell us (because we know what we are going to hear)? Because we are seeking confirmation, not information? Because what's being said is getting in the way of what *needs* to be said? Well they could certainly be some of the barriers to listening. Listening is in fact something we have to perform actively.

The advantages of listening are that your attention will be more focused on the matter at hand and you will get more information. If you listen, you can proceed with the task. It's interesting to observe some meetings where nobody is listening. The same data will come up again and again, in slightly different incarnations, and each person will make profound statements, only to be topped by the next person saying the same sort of thing. Nobody's learning anything, they're just making a bunch of speeches.

Geoff Nightingale of SynerGenics gives these 12 rules of listening:

1. Listen for ideas, not facts – ask yourself what they mean.

2. Judge content, not delivery, ie *what* they say, not how they say it.

3. Listen optimistically – don't lose interest straight away.

4. Do not jump to conclusions.

5. Adjust your note-taking to the speaker, ie be flexible.

6. Concentrate – don't start dreaming – and keep eye contact.

7. Do not think ahead of the speaker – you will lose track.

8. Work at listening – be alert and alive.

9. Keep emotions under control when listening.

10. Open your mind – practise accepting new information.

11. Breathe slowly and deeply.

12. Relax physically, get comfortable.

Active listening involves playing back your own interpretation of what has been said in acknowledgement – 'I see. Let me see if I understand you. As I see it, what you mean is . . . '

Way 56 Stay on track

It's very easy to allow a group of people to wander off in some strange direction. That's why it's important to have a competent facilitator who can obtain agreement on the purpose of the session, who can recognise when people begin to stray, and keep the direction going.

If you have just started defining the problem and some smartalick is already yelling out solutions, it's necessary to deliver the ground rules: 'Thank you, Fred. We'll be getting to that area soon. Meanwhile, why don't you write it down so we can deal with it when it's appropriate. Right now, we just want to concentrate on this specific area.'

Another way the group can get off track is to start trying to solve the wrong problem, which is why it's important to get agreement on the nature of the problem. 'Jim, that's a wonderful solution, but the problem we've agreed we're facing right now is this . . . Can you make that work for this?'

If you're in idea-generating mode and someone starts evaluating, point out that judgements will be made later. 'Joan, right now we're just identifying lots of ideas. We'll worry about how good they are shortly. How do you think this one you don't think will work could be *made* to work?'

And then there's the veiled warfare that can develop if a person has been allowed to dominate the session. Others get their weapons out, ready to scuttle the dominator at the first chance, and the track you're trying to follow becomes obscured in fog. If necessary, call a break and pull the offender aside for a quiet word, pointing out the purpose of the session and how it needs to be recovered. 'I need your help to make this happen. How can we give some of the other people a chance to participate?'

Way 57 Keep the group's energy up

After a while, the group can start to lose energy. You may have been working on a particularly difficult problem and seem to be getting nowhere. The room's getting stuffy. People are starting to yawn or slump over the table. It's time for a bit of a shake up!

This can be a physical activity. Get everybody to stand up and run on the spot for 30 seconds, or do stretches. Open the windows or turn up the air conditioning. Have everyone run around the quadrangle for a couple of minutes. Get some refreshments to replace the flagging body sugar.

Divert their attention for a few minutes with an excursion. This could be some silly little exercise, like identifying 50 uses for a paperclip or a tea bag. Or you could tell a joke, or play a videotape of something diverting and interesting – out-takes from your last TV commercial or corporate video get a lot of laughs. The idea is to blow the cobwebs out of their brains so that the group will start functioning efficiently again.

Way 58 Summarise, obtain agreement, allocate tasks

You should intend to complete the session in one go. It's not as effective to pick up and restart on another day. You should, of course, come back to deal with a side issue that may have developed.

When you started the session, you specified the objectives (they should also be in the briefing document). As you approach completion, you should summarise where you are, obtain everyone's agreement that this is the situation, and tasks should be allocated. You have all this quality stuff. Now who's going to deal with it? As I've pointed out, the job will be much simplified if a computer has been recording information during the session.

Techniques to Develop Solutions

Most of the techniques that follow work well in group sessions, and many can be employed if you're just doodling on your own. The techniques have been arranged in a reasonably logical sequence, so that you could, if you like, employ the ones that seem appropriate in that order. Some techniques need earlier techniques to have been performed before they can be carried out. But (And) don't get bogged down in this. These are idea prompters that have worked many times in many different situations. They are not *all* the answers. Feel free to modify and amend as you see fit.

Way 59 Understand your audiences' needs

As you begin your process of generating great ideas, it's important to have a clear understanding of *who* you're going to be taking the result to, when, and in what form.

There may well be several layers of audience. These could be:

- The people who asked you to work on the problem
- The people who pay your salary or bills
- The people who have to approve progressing the idea
- The people who will benefit from the solution
- The people who have to be involved to make the solution work
- The people at financial organisations such as banks
- The people who own shares in the company
- The people in the media who review what you're up to.

As to when you'll be dealing with these audiences, it could be:

- As soon as you have the result
- After it has been refined and processed a bit
- After it has been developed into a finished entity
- During its life
- After it's over.

Furthermore, the form in which you take the idea to the audience will vary. It might need:

- The back of an envelope, or the tablecloth from the restaurant where you hatched the idea
- A draft or formal document outlining the concept
- A personal presentation, perhaps with visuals, over-heads, slides, a video, mock-ups, renderings, brochures and the like
- Advertising and promotion
  - print, broadcast, direct mail, outdoor, point of purchase, displays
- Prototypes or production samples.

In Way 5, we looked at identifying the audiences/users/beneficiaries. Now we must *understand* them. Grouping the people from our Granby example in the above categories, we'd see:

Audience category	Audience	When	In what form
People who asked you to work on the problem	Advertising agency	As soon as formulated	Document & presentation
People who pay your salary or bills	Advertising agency	As soon as formulated	Document & presentation
People who have to approve it	Granby Aircraft Company	After it has been refined & processed	Document & presentation
People who will benefit from the solution	Advertising agency	As soon as formulated	Document & presentation
	Granby Aircraft Company	After it has been refined & processed	Document & presentation
	Granby dealers	After it has been developed into a finished entity	Document & presentation
	Granby aircraft owners	After it has been developed into a finished entity	Advertising & promotion
	Current other-brand aircraft owners. Licensed pilots, potential owners, new pilots	After it has been developed into a finished entity	Advertising & promotion
People who have to be involved to make the solution work	Advertising agency	As soon as formulated	Document & presentation
	Granby Aircraft Company	After it has been refined & processed	Document & presentation
	Granby dealers	After it has been developed into a finished entity	Document & presentation
	Granby aircraft owners	After it has been developed into a finished entity	Advertising & promotion
	Granby employees	After it has been developed into a finished entity	Document & presentation
People at financial organisations	No direct involvement, in this case	N/A	N/A
People who own shares in the company	Republic Steel Corporation	Regular management meeting	Document & presentation
People in the media	Aviation media	After it has been developed into a finished entity	Document & presentation

To be able to generate great ideas, then, you must know the audiences, understand their needs and be willing and able to serve them. You must know when you have to meet and talk with them. And you must know how you're going to do that.

Understanding your audience is not merely a matter of recognising that you have a certain number of critical groups. You must go beyond that. You must ask such questions as:

- 'What will *they* get from this idea?'
  - Not 'What will *we* get from this idea?'
- 'What do *they* want to hear from us?'
  - Not 'What do *we* want to tell them?'
- 'What can we do to help *them?*'
  - Not 'What can they do to help *us?*'

Way 60 Understand your objectives

The clearer your objective statement is, the better you will be able to devise strategies to achieve it.

A lot of people get the concepts of objectives and strategy mixed up. An *objective* is simply what you want to achieve. Start all statements of objective in the infinitive, and make them measurable:

- To generate at least 50 ideas that could help me solve the Granby problem
  (Not 'To solve the Granby problem').

A *strategy* is how you propose to achieve the objective. Start all statements of strategy with an active verb:

- Hold a brainstorming session

So the ideas you want to develop should flow from the strategies you identify to achieve the objectives. Like this:

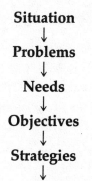

Situation
↓
Problems
↓
Needs
↓
Objectives
↓
Strategies
↓
Ideas Ideas Ideas Ideas Ideas Ideas Ideas Ideas Ideas

Way 61 What are they thinking now?

A good way to develop a better understanding of your audience is to find out what their present attitudes are. You can do this by:

- Talking to them informally
- Conducting research with them (see Way 6)
  - focus groups
  - personal interviews
  - telephone interviews
  - mail questionnaires
  - product-pack surveys
  - questionnaires printed or inserted in publications
- Asking your sales people or trade outlets
- Talking to the relevant media
- Talking to the competition
- Judgement.

If you're brainstorming each participant could be asked to write down what *they* think the audiences are thinking, then the results can be compared, reviewed, refined and recorded. A flipchart sheet hanging on the wall headed 'What Are They Thinking Now?' becomes a useful reference as the session continues.

Let's take our Granby example:

What Are They (Potential Buyers) Thinking Now?

- *Super aeroplane, pity about the price.*
- *I wish I could afford one, but costs have soared.*
- *The new Granby would do the job for me, but the annual cost is hard to justify - a third less would do the job.*
- *Too bad I can't rent one when I need it, but there's no operation near here that provides that service.*
- *I'm afraid to try one out, because I don't want to get into something I can't really afford.*
- *I wish there was a way I could afford one.*

Way 62 What do we want them to think?

If you can articulate in words what you would like your audiences to think about your idea, you'll be well on the way to producing it. (Bear in mind that what they *say* may be different from what they *think*.)

In your brainstorming session, ask each person to write down what they believe they'd like the audiences to be thinking. Then go over the results to arrive at a consensus. A wall-mounted flipchart sheet headed 'What Do We Want Them To Think?' helps the session to continue.

What Do We Want Them (Potential Buyers) To Think?

- *Super aeroplane, I'll go out of my way to have one.*
- *I'm prepared to make some sacrifices to have one.*

(Later)

- *Granby made it possible for me to have one.*
- *My new Granby does the job for me, I'm glad I have a way to operate it that I can afford.*
- *I'm glad I have a Granby.*

Way 63 What do we have to do to . . . ?

If you put the previous two ways together, you get to a logical question that demands an answer:

What Are They Thinking Now?

↓

What Do We Want Them To Think?

↓

What Do We Have To Do To Make Them Think That Way?

Look at the clues:

- *The new Granby would do the job for me, but the annual cost is hard to justify - a third less would do the job.*

- *I'm prepared to make some sacrifices to have one.*

↓

- *My new Granby does the job for me, I'm glad I have a way to operate it that I can afford.*

↓

☞ *What do we have to do to get them there?*

It seems we have to devise a way to reduce the cost of operation that doesn't involve too great a compromise.

Note the wording of the question. It's open-ended, to allow the broadest possibilities.

Q: *What do we have to do to make them think: 'The new Granby does the job for me, I'm glad I have a way to operate it that I can afford'?*

A: *Get the cost of operation down in a way that doesn't involve too great a compromise.*

And it prompts creative answers. You can keep asking it:

Q: *What do we have to do to get the cost of operation down in a way that doesn't involve too great a compromise?*

A: *1). Look at the costs and see how savings can be made.*
   2). Identify and evaluate possible compromises.

And keep asking it:

Q: What do we have to do to look at the costs?
A: 1). Identify the cost areas.
  2). Review possible savings ideas.

Thus this exercise points you at your strategy to solve the problem.

Way 64 What we need here is a strategy

A lot of people, as soon as they hear a problem, start shooting off ideas to solve it. But (And) the ideas can be all over the place. To develop ideas efficiently, you need a strategy that addresses the identified problem. If we didn't have a strategy for our Granby problem, we might have heard ideas like these:

Problem: We're not selling enough Granbys. What can we do?

- Run more ads
- Have a giveaway contest/lottery for buyers
- Cut the price so as to sell more planes and get the cost down
- Offer a free car with every plane
- Give big trade-in allowances
- Start a Hertz Rent-a-Plane programme
- Use a car engine that would be cheaper to buy and would use less and cheaper fuel instead of the expensive aero engine
- Subsidise the interest costs
- Lower the price of a plane by $20,000 and then announce the price goes up by $1000 a day if it's unsold
- Get someone to run a contest and offer Granbys as prizes

- Hold a contest for the dealers; the prize is a new Granby for top sales in three months
- Build the plane out of cheaper materials
- Build the plane out of recycled materials
- Build the plane in a country where labour costs are lower, etc.

Some of these ideas aren't bad. And if we had a *strategy*, we might get a more focused group of ideas. Well, we have a strategy that surfaced from our last exercise:

1). *Look at the costs and see how savings can be made.*
2). *Identify and evaluate possible compromises.*

☞ *List the costs:*

- Payments – say $3000 per month/$36,000 a year
- Storage (hangarage/parking) – say $2400 a year
- Fuel – say $25 a flying hour
- Insurance – say $3000 a year
- Annual inspection – say $1000
- Maintenance – say $10 a flying hour
- Reserve for engine overhaul – say $10 a flying hour.

Now we might start getting ideas like these:

☞ *What do we have to do to lower the costs?*

- Lobby for lower taxes on fuel, hangarage, etc
- Get government subsidy, tax allowances for business use of plane
- Charge use of plane to clients
- Get interest costs down
- Get storage costs down
- Get fuel costs down
- Get insurance costs down
- Get maintenance costs down

- Share the costs with other people.

☞ *Ooh, that gives me an idea! Share the costs with other people!*

- Get interest costs down – how?
- Get storage costs down – how?
- Get fuel costs down – how?
- Get insurance costs down – how?
  - Share the costs with other people!!!!

☞ *How can we share the costs with other people?*

See how the process works?

Way 65 Think vertically

There's nothing wrong with thinking vertically if you feel you are moving in the right direction. Here are some questions to ask about a problem that will help to develop a directional solution:

- Who is affected by the problem (make a list)
- Identify each type of effect and look for differences
- Describe the effect in at least three different ways
- See what solutions are suggested.

Let's try it with our favourite example:

- Who is affected by low Granby sales?
  - Granby Aircraft Company
  - Granby employees
  - Granby dealers
  - Advertising agency
  - Granby owners
  - Pilots who want a Granby
- Identify each type of effect and look for differences
  - Granby Aircraft Company
    Need to increase sales to maintain business

viability
Cannot reduce price without affecting profitability
- Granby employees
Business must get better or I could be laid off
- Granby dealers
New plane business must get better or I'm just going to deal in used aircraft
- Advertising agency
We could lose the account if we don't help solve the problem
- Granby owners
Healthy market for used Granbys, price is firm, good demand
Costlier to trade up to a new Granby
- Pilots who want a Granby
Expensive to get into a new Granby (or any new aircraft)
Maybe I can only afford a used aircraft.

Notice when you look through the above listing, you see several different types of problem.

- Whose business viability is threatened?
  - Granby Aircraft Company – worst
  - Advertising agency – not so bad (relatively small account)
- Who might have to change emphasis in their line of business?
  - Granby dealers
- Who isn't able to fly the kind of aircraft he or she wants?
  - Granby owners (older models)
  - Pilots who want a Granby
- Who is most threatened?
  - Granby Aircraft Company
  - Granby employees

- Who is least threatened?
  — Pilots who want a Granby
- Who does well anyway?
  — Granby dealers (healthy used aircraft market).

Now it's time to describe each impact in at least three different ways:

- Threat to business viability/most threatened
  - Bankruptcy
  - Fire sale
  - Predatory take over
- Change of business emphasis
  - Could improve profitability
  - Loss of specialised infrastructure
  - Need to retrain people
- Wrong kind of aircraft for pilot/least threatened
  - Less comfort, safety, prestige
  - Less satisfaction
  - More frustration
- Do well anyway
  - Less motivation to cooperate with new programme
  - You need me more than I need you
  - I'd like to increase my business by selling more new aircraft.

Now we want to see what solutions are suggested:

- To combat threat to business viability
  - Need to increase sales volume and maintain pricing
- To resist change of business emphasis
  - Need to maintain viability of existing product
- To correct wrong kind of aircraft for pilot problem
  - Need to find a way for them to be able to get the aircraft they really want

- To address those who do well anyway
  - Need to take advantage of their relative strength to help run the programme.

Now boil it down:

- Need to increase sales volume and maintain pricing structure, while maintaining the viability of the aircraft.
- Need to find a way for pilots to be able to get the aircraft they really want while taking advantage of dealer strength to help run the programme.

What does that suggest? How about this:

'Don't change the plane, change the way you sell it.'

Way 66 Define what success looks like

If you can project yourself forward into the future, you might think up a number of statements that would define the look of what you've achieved, assuming you made it successfully.

In a brainstorming session, the group could be asked to take five minutes to write out their own definitions of success. Then the facilitator asks each person to read out their ideas, while they are captured on the flipchart. If two ideas are identical, just indicate that – it's not necessary to write it out again. If you're getting a lot of input, it might be useful to have several flipcharts going and write the ideas down in categories as you go along. With eight people in the session, you should end up with perhaps 25-30 definitions.

Here are some examples of success definitions for our Granby case:

What does success look like?

- Sales have increased by 50 per cent

- They had to open another production line to keep up with demand
- We came up with a scheme that enabled buyers to acquire Granbys and spend a lot less money
- The Air Force bought 100 Granbys as trainers
- We're all over the media – on the front cover of the top three publications
- We were on network TV news last night with a positive story
- *The Wall Street Journal* did a very positive article about our scheme.

You may not immediately generate an idea out of this, and then again you may. And it's useful to have this page up on the wall, since you can point to it every so often. 'How can we make *this* happen?' you say, tapping one of the items. 'What do we have to do to get a positive story on network TV news?'

Way 67 What words of praise will be said?

Imagine that you have produced the idea that has solved the problem beyond all reasonable doubt. In fact, the problem has been solved so well, you are having a celebratory dinner at the finest restaurant in town. *You* solved the problem. Sitting across from you is your client. He looks at you with a big grin and raises his glass of Dom Perignon to toast you.

What are the words of praise he says?

The task here is to imagine a series of lines that the winner is saying about you and what you have done. Ideally, you should ask your *client* to do this for you. Give him the situation described above, and get him to fantasise. You will be amazed at the useful language that comes out, like:

'Thanks to that idea of buyers sharing the costs of operation, we sold a lot more aircraft in a tough market.'

'My sales director is complaining because he is selling it so quickly we're not making it fast enough. My boss said his wife likes the advertising – people look up to her at the country club. My competitors are gnashing their teeth because of the claims we've made that they can't make. Our customers are writing letters about the excellence of our service. The review in *The Wall Street Journal* really helped. *The Sunday Times* magazine ran it as the cover story. I was interviewed on Cable News Network.'

Collecting these lines might help you uncover some hidden objectives or concerns that could point you in precisely the right direction.

Way 68 List attributes

As part of the process of developing solutions, a good technique is to list the attributes of the device, the problem or the solution, and see what comes up. In the case of the Granby 400 aeroplane, these attributes include:

- It flies at speeds up to 325 kmph
- It has four seats and dual sets of controls, so two pilots can fly it
- It is made of metal (mostly aluminium and steel)
- It has a four-cylinder, air-cooled engine that develops 149 kW
- It weighs 1243 kg when loaded
- It carries 242 litres of fuel
- It cost (at the time of our case) about $120,000 when fully equipped
- It has a laminar flow wing
- Its wing spar is made in one piece for great strength
- It measures 10.67 m span by 7.52 m long by 2.54 m high

- It will stay in the air for over 6.6 hours at normal cruising speed
- It will fly up to 1800 km without refuelling
- It can be equipped with weather radar and full instrumentation for all-weather flight
- It is positioned as an owner-flown, high-performance method of transportation
- Almost all owners use the aircraft for personal transportation.

Now if you go back and look over these attributes, certain items point to an idea. They are these:

- *It has four seats and dual sets of controls, so two pilots can fly it*
- *It will stay in the air for over 6.6 hours at normal cruising speed*
- *It can be equipped with weather radar and full instrumentation for all-weather flight*
- *It is positioned as an owner-flown, high-performance piece of transportation equipment*
- *Almost all owners use the aircraft for personal transportation.*

The idea? *Position the aircraft as a trainer* to teach pilots high-performance instrument flying. (Granby subsequently did this and sold quite a few aircraft to airline flight schools.)

The more attributes you can think of, the more useful they will be. We tend to prejudge situations based upon past experience, or the way something seems. Granbys had always been sold as personal, owner-flown aircraft. The idea of repositioning a version as a trainer had not been avidly pursued. Everybody knows that trainers are simple little two-seaters. You don't teach people to fly in complex aeroplanes. And when Granby bit the bullet and painted an aircraft to look like a trainer, equipped it with a more utilitarian interior and set up an attractive price based upon quantities and standard equipment, and *called* it an instrument trainer, it worked. They got orders because they went after the business and asked for them.

All right. Take five minutes and list the attributes of a ping-pong ball. Then identify as many other-than-normal uses for it as you can. Or do the same with:

- A glass milk bottle
- A bathroom-cabinet mirror
- A household paintbrush
- A credit card
- A garden fork
- A brick
- An empty tea bag
- A paperclip
- A 35mm film cassette, etc.

Way 69 Make a statement

Notice in the last item I said 'when Granby bit the bullet, and *called* it an instrument trainer, it worked'. A lot of success in getting to places you want to be has to do with what you *say*. People tend to accept what you say, especially if you look or sound convincing. A couple of years ago, when making my video *Your Guide to Antique Shopping in Britain,* I needed to arrange, usually on short notice, to get into some location with a camera crew so we could record an interview or some action on vid-eotape. I found the best technique was to start the telephone conversation with these words: 'Hello. I am a television producer. We're making a programme about antiques and I'd like to bring a camera crew in to shoot some scenes tomorrow afternoon . . . ' The magic words were 'I am a television producer'. I had a baseball cap from some TV company which had their logo on the front. I'd wear that going into the location for the first meeting. 'Oh, Mr Fizbee, the television people are here!'

How can you pull off a new idea? Make the appropriate statement about it. (It has to be true and believable, but [and] it needs to be said.) And while you're just at the idea-generating stage, you are *allowed to say anything about anything*. You have *permission*. When I started to write *The Aircraft Owner's Handbook*, I very quickly appended the subtitle *Everything You Need to Know About Buying, Operating and Selling an Aircraft*. Now I *knew* what I had to do.

When I was asked to make a video about the history of the car, I baulked. The objective was to put together an interesting story using a vast library of archive film footage. I don't know enough about cars to make a video called *Wheels – The History of the Car*. Some car buffs would be sure to write in and say 'You left out the most important thing, which is . . . ' So I got the client to agree to call it *Wheels – The Joy of Cars*. Now we were working to *my* rules. I could go anywhere the footage led me. And we made a nice little video.

Way 70 Make up a solution

Back to our Granby case. You'll notice we were beginning to get somewhere. We had evolved a strategy (Ways 63 and 64).

Q: *What do we have to do to get the cost of operation down in a way that doesn't involve too great a compromise?*

A: *1). Look at the costs and see how savings can be made*
    2). Identify and evaluate possible compromises.

And a challenge . . .

☞ *How can we share the costs with other people?*

So now we're moving towards being able to make up a solution and see how it sounds. How could people share the costs of ownership?

- They could form a flying club and buy a plane, then share the costs of operation. Twelve people could put up $10,000 each. Or by financing it, have a monthly payment of $300 each.
- They could form a partnership of maybe two or three people and buy a plane.

Both of these ideas are hardly new. They've been around since aeroplanes were first offered to the public. And they are in the right direction, because an effective programme of this type would work. How can we make it Granby's?

- Granby could offer to build a database of people interested in sharing ownership – you register with us, we introduce you to other people who want to do the same thing in your area
- We'd give it a name and announce it as a whole marketing programme.

The act of devising a solution begins to bring it to life. It needs to be made whole, and to do this, it requires a simple developmental technique. This technique should be foolproof and demand answers. One that I use all the time is to write out a description of the solution using three simple headings:

- What it is
- How it works
- What it does.

In this way, I find I can write a clear outline, and the act of doing this enables me to identify gaps that must be filled. Let's try it with our Granby example:

Granby's Share the Costs of Ownership Scheme

- What it is
  - Marketing scheme offered by Granby to sell their aircraft

- – Provides ways for prospective purchasers to identify others with whom they could enter into a shared ownership operation
- – Shows them how to do it
- How it works
  - – Granby announces scheme
    - – Advertising
    - – Brochure explaining idea
  - – Granby builds database of prospects
    - – Identifies people interested in sharing in various locations
  - – Granby introduces potential prospects to each other
    - – Dealer activities, seminars
- What it does
  - – Eases task of people wanting to share ownership in a Granby
  - – Enables customers to acquire interest in a valuable transport asset at considerable savings
  - – Demonstrates Granby leadership
  - – Granby could 'own' the concept, pre-empting competition.

See how it works?

Way 71 Identify the needs that flow from the solution

Our technique in Way 70 helps to lay out the solution in a manner that others (who may not have been in the preliminary meetings) can understand. You could go a long way with just the information that comes up when you use that method.

And to progress it further, it would be good to identify the needs that come up from the description. Let's take a look at what the Granby programme suggested:

Needs

- A good name for the programme: *Granby's Share the Costs of Ownership Scheme* won't fly
- A way to introduce the scheme to its audiences
- A system for taking registrations of people interested
- A database to manage it
- A brochure that explains it
- A way to get the dealers involved
- A way to introduce the potential prospects.

Each of these needs then requires work to develop it. What we eventually came up with was:

- A name: *The Granby Time-Sharing Plan*
- An advertising programme, with a mail-in coupon on which people could register, plus a tent at Oshkosh, the world's most important general aviation show, where we made live presentations about the plan and took registrations
- A video introducing the plan, and a slide show explaining it
- A computerised matching system (like computer dating, matched up by desired operating base)
- A 20-page *Granby Time-Sharing Manual*
- A series of seminars put on at dealerships, where registrants attended, were introduced to each other and presentations were made explaining the programme.

The result? In the few months it ran (until Granby changed management and agencies, it became 'not invented here' and died) five were sold. You have to give a great idea like that time to work!

Way 72 Use a dictionary and a thesaurus

You may have noticed that once in a while a dictionary definition is given in this book. This is a very useful technique for clarifying a point and making sure that we're all on the same wavelength. However, in any kind of idea generation activity, reference to a dictionary or thesaurus will provide all sorts of help.

When you're defining a problem, and you've come up with some words to do that, look the words up in the dictionary and see what you get. Look up the words that define the words. Make a new definition using these words. Let's try one at random:

Hypothesis An unproved theory; proposition; supposition
Unproved Untested; untried
Theory An idea or mental plan of the way to do something
Proposition Proposal; plan
Supposition Something supposed; theory; hypothesis (Ha!)
Proposal Plan; scheme
Plan Scheme for making, doing or arranging something; project; proposal
Idea Plan; scheme; project
Scheme Carefully arranged and systematic plan of action
Project A proposal of something to be done; scheme

That could all lead to the following definition:
Hypothesis: An untested, untried idea or mental plan or proposal or scheme of the way to do or arrange something.

The words *untested* or *untried* might give you more insight into the problem than just the word *unproven*. The words *idea, mental plan, proposal* or *scheme* might help you more than just the word *theory*.

Look up *hypothesis* in a thesaurus and you get words like: principle, premise, philosophy, surmise, belief, opinion, persuasion, sentiment, point of view, stand, position, attitude, and so on. The technique is to see how these words affect your understanding of the problem, how they make your mind move, where they take you. What words do these words conjure up?

Way 73 Word associate

Take the definition of the problem and identify the key words in it. In our Granby example, the definition (see Way 10) was:

- How can we increase sales of a quality, speciality product (personal aeroplane) that qualified people want very much but basically can no longer afford to own?

The key words are:

- Increase sales
- Quality
- Speciality product
- Personal aeroplane
- Qualified people
- Want very much
- Can no longer afford to own.

Now do a word association on each set of key words (you should do at least twice or thrice as many as there are here):

- *Increase sales.* Build volume, ring the cash register, laugh all the way to the bank, improve the bottom line, make more money, success, bonus, rewards.
- *Quality.* Good, best, well made, prestigious, expensive, get what you pay for, long life, solid.
- *Speciality product.* Rare, specialised, unusual, unique appeal, dedicated application, envy generator.
- *Personal aeroplane.* Off we go into the wild blue yonder, my own set of wings, freedom, three dimensions, time saver, fun, pleasure.

- *Qualified people.* Pilot's licence, special, rare, identifiable, similarity of attitude towards flying, positive quality, proud of ticket, good pilot, handle complex situations, gives me the edge, need to practise, build my hours, soar in the sky.
- *Want very much.* Desirable, envy, lust, eat your heart out, demand, earned, pilot's right to greatness in transportation.
- *Can no longer afford to own.* Make more money, make sacrifices, work it out, there must be a way, what do I have to do to own one?

Do you see how ideas start coming up? Look at the solution we evolved for Granby (see Ways 70 and 71). Notice how many of these words point to that solution?

You get what you pay for, long life, solid, unique appeal, my wings, freedom, gives me the edge, need to practise, pilot's right to greatness in transportation, make sacrifices, work it out, there must be a way, what do I have to do to own one?

The answer? Granby Time Sharing!

Way 74 Do a word association ring around

A good way to play word association with a group and keep up a high level of energy is to do a 'ring around'. The facilitator picks a word (perhaps at random, perhaps a key word you've been working on), then goes around the room as fast as possible asking each person in turn to say a word suggested by the last word they heard. This should be done by pointing at each person in turn, and having them respond instantly, with each word being written down on the flipchart (it helps to have a separate scribe to record the words).

You can do this with several different key words, looking for 30 or more words per cue. After a few minutes of this, when you have many words, stop the action and run down the words to see what has come up in the way of idea prompters.

Way 75 Build on ideas, combine ideas (stepping stones)

If you're in a group, here's a technique that can be quite helpful. The facilitator asks everyone to focus on a particular aspect of the agreed problem. Each person is to take a piece of paper and write an idea on it. They do this as many times as possible, writing each idea on a separate sheet. When they've finished each idea, they put the piece of paper in the centre of the table. So fairly soon there is a pile of ideas in the kitty. When someone dries up they take one of the sheets from the kitty (other than one of their own), and look at what someone else has written. Then they propose modifications, extensions, improvements and refinements of what they see there. When they've finished, they put it back in the kitty and pick another one to work on.

Let this process happen for maybe 20-30 minutes. Then gather the sheets all together and deal them out, like playing cards. Then ask each person to read out an idea in turn, while someone captures the essence of these on the flipchart. Do this until all the ideas are recorded.

Way 76 Relate the matter to a picture of a person

This is a quick way to evaluate a proposition from various points of view. Start by stating the proposition – maybe it's an idea that has just come up, maybe it's the actual problem you're working on. The facilitator should have assembled a number of pictures of people from various sources – magazines, advertisements and the like. The pictures should be as neutral as possible – not someone sitting in a sports car or sipping a glass of Chivas Regal –

more like a passport picture. They should be of various types of person:

- Men and women (children, if relevant)
- Different ages (teens, 20s, 30s, 40s, 50s, 60s, 70s+)
- Different ethnic groups
- Various types of attire (business suit, casual, leisure).

The facilitator deals a picture to each person in the group who has to make up a story about the person depicted (name, where they live, occupation, values) and asks them to tell the group how this person would respond to the proposition being studied.

In this way you'll get some good thinking prompted by the stereotypes the people have identified.

Way 77 Be outrageous or provocative and see what you get

To get away from stereotypes, using the same sorts of picture as in Way 76, try this. Deal them out and ask the people to make up an outrageous or provocative story about their picture. Why does this man have his picture in the tabloids? What did he do? The assignment is to be as way out as possible. Then ask them to tell the group how this person, in the light of this event, would respond to the proposition being studied.

Way 78 Look at parallel problems/solutions/ analogies

Define the problem, then ask each person to suggest an analagous problem. 'What is this problem like? What's the parallel?' Give them perhaps five or ten minutes to do this (they should write it down), then ask each person to read out their analogy. Pick one of these and work out solutions to *that* problem. Spend maybe 20 minutes on this, then see if you can relate these solutions back to your *real* problem.

Way 79 Suggest a metaphor for the problem

This is another way of looking at Way 78. My dictionary defines *metaphor* as 'a figure of speech in which one thing is likened to another; a different thing being spoken of as if it were that other; implied comparison in which a word or phrase ordinarily or primarily used of one thing is applied to another (eg, screaming headlines)'. The task is to suggest a metaphor for the problem. Get the group to do it. Then see what the metaphors suggest. Here are some metaphors relevant to the case we've been studying:

> 'goes like a bat out of hell'
> 'flies like a homesick angel'
> 'soars like an eagle'
> 'equipped like a 747'
> 'built like a tank with wings'
> 'costs as much as a house'
> 'handles as smooth as silk'
> 'handles like a fighter'.

Way 80 Look at a picture and relate it to the problem

Use a slide projector to show a series of really beautiful colour photographs. One might be of some wondrous example of nature – a waterfall in the mountains, a sunset, a line of thunderclouds, a desert or jungle scene. Another might be of an animal or a building. Or something powerful, like a jet fighter taking off from a carrier, or a steam train at full speed.

Leave each image on the screen for one minute, and ask the group to think about the problem while looking at the picture and write down what comes into their heads as a result.

Way 81 Develop action phrases and apply them

Ask the group to take five minutes each to write down 20 action phrases that could be applied to solving the problem. Then record them on the flipchart, apply the words and see what you get.

The kinds of phrase you want them to give you are these:

- Make it larger
- Make it smaller
- Change the colour
- Cut the price
- Change the package
- Sell it differently, etc.

Way 82 Pick a word and relate it to the problem

You'll ideally need a dictionary, but in fact any book with a lot of words in it will do. Open the book at random and stab your finger on a word. Say the word out loud. Everybody has to write down what that word suggests when linked to the problem.

Do this perhaps a dozen times, until you get bored. Don't stop if you think you've got a good idea out of it. Keep going – there's more where that came from.

There is a Canadian gadget called Think Tank. It's a white plastic 10-inch sphere with a 4-inch diameter window in it. Inside the sphere are 32,000 words, each one on a separate chip of plastic. The sphere has a knob on each side that, when twisted, churns up the contents inside. Thus at any time, you can see maybe 20 words through the window. Churn away, and there are 20 more. It's for finding random words. Here are the words it showed when I churned it just now: implication, jukebox, baguette, coaxial, dextrose, shirk, impiety, saleability, bushel, willpower, shatter. Get any ideas?

Way 83 Be the competition and plan to kill you

Once I was running a brainstorming session in which we were thinking up ways to introduce New Coca-Cola to Europe (ultimately it never happened). I suggested to the group that we pretend we were Pepsi Cola Europe. How would we combat the introduction of New Coke? What would we expect Coca-Cola to do and what would we do to scuttle their plans?

By wearing the competition's hat we were able to look at the problem from a different perspective, resulting in lots of interesting ideas.

Way 84 What if you do nothing?

One choice you have in planning a series of actions is *not* to act. Take a look at this approach in the light of your problem. Ask the group to write down the consequences of no action. Then have them read them out and record them on the flipchart. Look at the consequences, and see whether, if *they* were reversed, would they suggest an idea for handling the task? Or maybe doing nothing makes sense!

Way 85 Reverse the situation, then reverse the solution

Define the situation in as reverse a manner as possible. Whatever is there, state it as the opposite. Redefine the problem. Look at solutions suggested by the reversed problem, then reverse the new solution. Does that give you new insights into the challenge?

'Granby Aircraft are selling three times as many planes as they did a couple of years ago. Factories are running three shifts and there is a shortage of raw materials to build the aeroplane. Dealers are complaining about huge waiting lists and bargaining among purchasers to get up the list more quickly. Competition is trying to keep up and is beginning to steal away customers. The company have lowered the price of the aircraft, due to production savings, but this has only served to increase demand.'

What kind of problem does this suggest? How about: 'How can we not lose sales of our quality speciality product (personal aeroplane) that is selling so well and that qualified people are impatient to buy?'

What kind of solution does this suggest? Why not use some of the techniques described here and see what emerges?

Then reverse the solution and see if you get any new ideas.

Way 86 Redefine the problem

After a long period of ideating, you might be ready for a change. Try redefining the problem. Ask the group to take three minutes and redefine the agreed problem, and see what you come up with. Here was our original one:

'How can we increase sales of a quality speciality product (personal aeroplane) that qualified people want very much but basically can no longer afford to own?'

How about these:

Redefined problem	Suggested solutions
How can we get more people interested in buying a Granby	Learn-to-fly programme
	Schools programme
	Airline pilots programme
	Military pilots programme
How can we sell more Granbys?	Look for other markets, other uses
	- Military training
	- National rent-a-plane network
	Develop innovative financing packages that lower cost of acquisition

What else could we do with our factory and experienced engineers, so that we can stay a viable business, given that we have very limited research capital?	Look for subcontracting work in the aerospace industry Design a lower-cost aircraft

Now look at the solutions suggested and see if any of these would work as part of or as a modification to what you are working on.

'Develop innovative financing packages that lower cost of acquisition' sounds interesting. Something that has as long a life as a private aeroplane (easily ten years or more) should have a high retained value (look at the strength in the current used market). Is there any way we can work out some kind of lease, like they have with expensive cars?

'Airline pilots scheme' could have some value. They make a lot of money, they know how to fly and they like well-equipped aeroplanes. Could we develop a programme for pilots who like to commute to their base airports? Maybe a group of them could own one together.

Way 87 When you get bogged down, take a mental excursion

If you keep working away at the same problem, grind, grind, grind, you might find yourself getting frustrated and angry. You may feel you're blocked. These are not always good sentiments to have when you're trying to generate great ideas.

The time has come to go on a mental excursion. You want to shake the cobwebs out a bit by shifting your intentions. Change the dynamics of the situation. Everybody change seats. Someone else be the facilitator. Give the group a totally new assignment. Spend perhaps 20 minutes on a different type of problem:

- Solve some current challenge
  - Oil pollution problems
  - Global warming
  - Recycling
- Solve some problem at work
  - New business ideas
  - What to do with unused office space
  - How to expand workload within existing space/ employee-count limitations
- Solve some hypothetical problem
  - How to defy gravity
  - Uses for the NASA Space Shuttle.

Suppose we were intending to propose a way to launch a new product – a new type of carbonated soft drink: fizzy tomato juice. For years the beverage industry has been unable to create carbonated tomato juice effectively because the liquid is too viscous. But now, thanks to scientific research, a breakthrough has occurred. New *power bubbles* work even with thick juice. And you don't have to shake the can, because the bubbles keep it mixed up properly. What do you do to get it going?

Way 88 Draw a picture/flow chart

Thinking graphically can help to identify problem areas you may not have detected when looking at the situation as a simple write up. Think about how you could depict the development in images or as a series of steps in a diagram or table. (See the Ways indicated for examples.)

- Cartoons with or without speech bubbles (see Way 38)
- Presentation slides
- Flow chart (see Way 60)
- Chronological chart/time lines/timetable (see Way 45)
- Computer screen shots (see Way 19)

- Tabulation of information (see Ways 4, 49, 59, 93)
- Tabulation of numbers (see Way 92)
- Resource chart
- Organisation chart
- Schematic diagram (see Way 41)
- Maps/plans (see Way 46)

Another technique to illustrate a point is to use a quotation from a relevant work (see Way 16).

Way 89 Will it make money?

It's easy to get carried away, and that's what we want to do for the major part of a creative development session. Money should be no object for a long time. But (And) there comes a moment when some hard realities must be faced. What is the answer to the question 'Will it make money?' And if the answer is 'Maybe not much,' then ask the second part of the question: 'What do we have to do to make it make money?' The answers to this may give you a part of the solution you've been looking for.

Way 90 Turn obstacles into opportunities

When you're near completion, identify the obstacles to success, then see how they can be turned into opportunities. Perhaps you make a list of possible customer objections, and produce the statement that overcomes the objection. The point is, you want to have your idea as solid as possible when you're ready to take it further.

It might help to have a table laid out like this:

Possible objection	Suggested response
Too complicated	We have trained advisers and a comprehensive manual to handle all questions, *supported by a 24-hour hotline*

For example, the last part of the response, 'supported by a 24-hour hotline' was not in the original idea, but it came up as a result of doing this exercise.

Way 91 Challenge assumptions

As you approach the evaluative segment of your programme of developing great ideas, put on a challenging hat. Be the unimpressed bank manager or board director who asks the awkward questions. Here are some tough questions to ask:

- Why do you think this will work?
- Is this the best solution to the problem?
- Has anyone else tried this? What happened for/to them?
- Why should we bother with this?
- Who needs it?
- What if you don't do it?
- Suppose it costs twice as much as you've budgeted. What will you do then?
- What does the sales force think?
- What do the trade/distributors think?
- What do/will our customers think?
- Have our customers seen this yet?
- How firm is your timetable? Suppose there were delays, what would they do?
- Can you think of a better use for the money/resources/time?
- Do we really need this?
- What will the media think?
- Are there any regulatory problems?
- What are the unknowns?

- What assumptions have you made, and on what basis?
- What chances are there of this being a hit?
- What about competition?
- Are you going to advertise this? How?
- What is your advertising creative approach?
- Will you need additional funding before this comes to fruition?
- Why should I put my neck on the line for this?
- Do you have any misgivings?
- Do you like this yourself?
- Should we do this?

Techniques to Measure Ideas

It's all very well to generate a whole raft of ideas. But (And) now we get to the evaluation part. We switch brain sides and go from right-brain thinking to left-brain thinking. On the next few pages, you'll find a number of techniques to measure and evaluate the ideas you've generated to separate the great from the not-so-great.

As pointed out in Way 13, you should allocate a specific time to this process. Don't evaluate while you ideate!

Way 92 Group ideas and rank them

Now you have all these scrawls on the walls, you need to make some sense of them. This is where a computer idea organiser (see Way 19) is so useful. Whether you have one or must do it manually, the process now is to assemble all the ideas in each particular category (categories could be, for example: 'Product introduction', 'Sales force ideas', 'Trade ideas', 'Publicity ideas', 'Lobbying ideas', 'Quality control ideas'), and then put them into an order of preference within each category.

You could ask the group to take a few minutes to rank each idea within a category (1 is first, 2 is second, etc), then report in. Let's say there are five ideas in Category A. The rankings come in from the six people in the room. Make a table like that overleaf to gather votes from the group. As Joe calls out his ranking of preferences for each idea, enter the figures vertically. Then enter May's set vertically. Then Sam's, and so on. Finally you'll have six sets of figures for each idea. Then add the figures across to get a total. The smallest resultant figure is thus ranked first by consensus, the next smallest second, and so on.

IDEAS EVALUATION SHEET								
IDEA	RANKINGS						RESULT	
Category A	Joe	May	Sam	Ed	Jill	Jim	SCORE	RANK
Idea 1	3	2	3	1	3	4	16	3
Idea 2	2	1	2	2	2	3	12	2
Idea 3	5	5	4	4	5	5	28	5
Idea 4	1	3	1	3	1	2	11	1
Idea 5	4	4	5	5	4	1	23	4

FINAL RANKING:		SCORE
1	Idea 4	11
2	Idea 2	12
3	Idea 1	16
4	Idea 5	23
5	Idea 3	28

Note that in this instance, ideas 4 and 2 were very close, so they probably both merit further attention. The last three ideas should probably be set aside. Do the same process for each category.

Way 93 Look at the pros and cons

If you're having trouble judging in which direction to go, a good technique to help is the pros and cons listing.

Take our Granby example, and look at individual aircraft ownership, versus co-owning an aircraft with other people. (In the table below, the pros and cons should be read vertically – a con across from a pro is not necessarily related to that pro.)

Pros of individual ownership	Cons of individual ownership
• You can pick exactly the aircraft you want	• High hourly cost with low utilisation
• You can equip it exactly as you want	• You have capital or credit tied up

- You can use it whenever you want to

- You can make full use of any tax benefits from business use

- It's yours and yours alone

- You have pride of ownership

- You are responsible for compliance with airworthiness and maintenance requirements

- Aircraft may lie fallow for long periods if you don't fly often

Pros of co-ownership

- Sharing fixed expenses (acquisition, insurance, storage, annual inspection) brings cost of operation down to lower levels that are easier to justify

- Your hourly cost is a lot lower, even with low utilisation

- You can pick exactly the aircraft you want

- You can equip it exactly as you want

- You can use it almost whenever you want to

- You always know who flew it last

- You can share tax benefits from business use

- You can practise your flying skills with your partner as safety pilot

- You have pride of ownership

Cons of co-ownership

- You need one or more compatible partners

- You have capital or credit tied up

- Aircraft may not always be available when you want it

- You are jointly responsible for compliance with airworthiness and maintenance requirements

- Low-experience partner may drive insurance costs high

Don't throw this kind of thinking out! The above thoughts eventually became a part of the marketing programme, by forming a component of the explanatory brochure.

Way 94 Write the ad that sells the result

Whether or not you will eventually use an advertisement, write the one that would sell the result of your thinking. It will help to crystallise your concepts. When I had the idea for *The Aircraft Owner's Handbook* it came to me whole. I saw the complete structure, who it was aimed at, what it was designed to do – everything – in one go. I got the idea one Sunday morning, after an early morning joy ride and immediately sat down and wrote a four-page direct-mail letter that would sell the book to prospective aircraft owners. The act of writing the letter confirmed the idea for the book and drove it forward.

Here are the first few paragraphs of the letter:

Dear Aircraft Owner:

I'm sure you'll agree that owning an aeroplane should be fun, not a constant source of irritation. That's what I thought – yet I kept finding more problems than fun, after I bought my plane.

I looked around for the one book that would help me. The book that would answer all my questions. It didn't exist! So I had to keep finding out the idiosyncrasies of aircraft ownership on my own. I delved and foraged. I was an inquisitive pain in the neck. Always snooping around when they worked on my plane. Looking in the radio shop when the avionics were out of it. Touring the aircraft factories and writing to people, etc.

Later I showed the letter to a friend who worked for a publisher. She said 'This is the sort of book we do. I'd like to show this to my boss.' The result? I made a presentation on the book, got a contract and advance, and finished writing it in six months.

It all came from having a clear idea of what the book was intended to do, and that came from that simple four-page letter.

Way 95   Write the headlines that report the solution

As part of your evaluation technique, put some journalistic skills to work to show how the solution will be reported in the press. What headlines would you like to see? What sub-heads? In what publications? Is there a particular writer you would like to see bylining the story? How would you like to see him or her treat it?

Do this from several points of view:

- The business press
- Quality newspapers
- Tabloid newspapers
- Trade publications
- Special-interest media
- General interest magazines/Sunday supplements
- Broadcast media
- International media

Don't just write a praiseworthy treatment. Compose a variety of critical approaches. What are the negatives? How might they be handled?

As an expansion of this technique, it might even be worthwhile role-playing some interviews with journalists. There are many agencies that provide 'media training' (for example most public relations agencies do this). This is a process in which one or more of your spokespeople go through intensive rehearsals with real journalists to learn how to handle a variety of interviews, ranging from straight information-gathering to typically journalistic probes (raising a variety of opposing issues), to blatantly antagonistic panel discussions.

Way 96 Do another SWOT analysis

The technique described in Way 8, an analysis of Strengths, Weaknesses, Opportunities and Threats, not only works when you're trying to isolate the problem. It also helps you evaluate your solution.

Before you finalise everything, conduct a further SWOT analysis, this time on the proposed solution, and see what further refinements are suggested. You may get some fresh ideas on introducing the solution to the public, communicating to the sales force or dealers, or dealing with potential competition.

Way 97 Do mock-ups and research the results

The more realistic the characterisation of the idea, the better you can check it out in advance. It's hard for many people to imagine what you mean from a description, or even an artist's impression. Or maybe they'll be so good at it that their impression is quite different from what you intend. Far better if you can build a mock-up of the solution, ideally full scale.

It could be that ergonomics are involved. Do the knobs and controls come comfortably to hand? Or do you have to twist around while using three separate hands to operate three simultaneously needed buttons?

Thanks to CAD (computer-aided design), many concepts can be tested out on the screen at relatively low cost. You can see how the building will look from different viewpoints. You can look at the view from different floors. You can see how an office will lay out, or a production line will operate.

Whatever you do, something more than a few words on a piece of paper will help you to make sure the solution will work.

Way 98 Why could it fail? Look at its flop potential

Take what you hope is an uncharacteristically pessimistic point of view and imagine the worst. Abject failure. Why will your brilliant solution flop? What is the worst thing that could happen? What would cause it? What would be the consequences? What are the barriers to success? Here are some examples:

- Production delays
- Errors in development
- Catastrophe (fire, earthquake, war)
- Weather problems (too hot/too cold/too wet/too dry/too windy)
- Strikes/industrial action
- Cost overruns
- Competitive pre-emption
- Changes in laws (regulation/taxes)
- Financial problems
- Staff training problems
- Business failure of distributor or retailer
- Economic conditions (high unemployment/interest rates/stock-market crash)
- Poor advertising results
- Public apathy

Sorry. I know this is painful, but someone's got to do it. Better you should find out now than after the big money's been spent.

Way 99 State and rank the core benefits

People don't buy products, they buy benefits. Consumers don't buy a stereo, they buy 'beautiful sound'. They don't buy a video recorder, they buy 'freedom to watch TV on their own terms'. What we need to do is identify the core benefits.

The core benefit is the most compelling reason to accept your proposition, based on a specific feature. How can you recognise a benefit from a feature, and get to the core benefit?

Here's my method. It is based on the word *so*. All you do is make a statement about the product or service, and then say 'so?' There needs to be a slight questioning inflection in your voice. And you keep saying 'so?' until you get to the ultimate benefit.

For example: 'This video recorder (VCR) has its own tuner, so? You can record a programme on one channel while you are watching one on another channel, so? You can run your life on your own terms, not on the dictates of a programme schedule, so? You can get more out of your time, and do what you want when you want, so? You can be free, so?' When you run out of responses to the word 'so?', you should be at the ultimate benefit.

Gather together a selection of core benefits for your solution, then rank them in order of importance.

Way 100 Conduct a reality check

It may seem proper to dream away in your garrett or back room, maintaining absolute secrecy at all times until the moment you reveal the solution. And will it fly when it gets out into the real world?

When Coca-Cola introduced New Coke in the USA in the mid '80s, it was done after exhaustive research that showed, time and again, people preferred the taste of the new formula to good old Coke. So, with the expenditure of millions, New Coke was launched and old Coke was discontinued. There was a public outcry. 'What have you done with our Coca-Cola?' What the researchers had not checked was the answer to the question 'Would you be happy if this was the flavour of Coca-Cola, *and you could no longer buy the current Coke?*' Good old Coke was quickly reintroduced as Coke Classic, and plans to launch New Coke in the rest of the world were shelved.

A few years earlier there were two new videodisk systems in development. One incorporated a laser beam reading a series of microscopic pits in the disk (Pioneer). This is similar to today's compact disk technology. The other incorporated a needle – like a record player – riding in a microgroove (RCA). Which system do you think failed in the market-place? How difficult do you suppose it would have been to predict that failure? Surely anyone could tell that a system based on old-fashioned record-player technology would not appeal? How many vinyl LP records are produced today? RCA could have saved $5 billion.

Reality checks are certainly worthwhile. They involve talking to independent people who don't have anything riding on the result, or customers, perhaps in a focus group (see Way 7). Talk to the sales force, the distributors, the readers of the magazine, suppliers. Obviously, this may have to be done with great care to preserve confidentiality. Don't just rely on your own judgement. If you've been working on an idea for months, you'll have a love/hate relationship with it. You cannot possibly be objective about it.

Way 101 Don't stop when you've finished

Just because you've come up with a solution, won approval to proceed, obtained the funding, produced the result and launched it doesn't mean you should stop there. You have to keep refining the result, in the light of experience in the real world. If you do it right, you can keep going for ages. If you do it wrong, the competition will eat you alive. Why? Because nobody's perfect. No matter how brilliant your solution, and how many changes you engineered before it was finally launched, when it does appear in the market-place, it could still stand improvement. If you don't make the improvements, someone else will.

Look at how long the Volkswagen Beetle was on the market, and how it changed over the years. How about the Boeing 747?

Here's an exercise. Think of what innovative products or services have been introduced in the last 20 years or so that have been superseded by a superior competitive venture.

The challenge of continual upgrading and improvement should keep you going. The problem is quite simple. Consumers have expectations. Innovators produce exciting solutions, sometimes so far ahead of expectations that minds are collectively blown – for a few moments. For no sooner has the solution arrived than consumer expectations move ahead. So innovators address these new expectations, and, with luck, exceed them. The consumer looks at it and says, 'That's nice. But wouldn't it be nicer if it did *this*, as well?' They're never satisfied.

Neither should you be. Keep generating great ideas. Keep one step ahead of your market-place. And while you're using this book to help, I'll be working on the 'new, improved edition'!

Further Reading From Kogan Page

Understanding Problems

A Handbook of Market Research Techniques, Robin Birn, Paul Hague & Phyllis Vangelder

Systematic Problem-Solving and Decision-Making, Sandy Pokras

Business Marketing Research, The Industrial Market Research Association

Understanding the Mind

Mind Mapping and Memory, Ingemar Svantesson

Building Your Own Creativity

The Art of Creative Thinking, John Adair

The Challenge of Innovation, John Adair

Generating Ideas in Groups

A Practical Guide to Effective Listening, Diane Bone

Effective Meeting Skills, Marion E Haynes

Effective Presentation Skills, Steve Mandel

How to Communicate Effectively

How to Make Meetings Work, Malcolm Peel

Icebreakers, Ken Jones

The Facilitators' Handbook, John Heron

Techniques to Develop Solutions

Creative Thinking in Business, Carol Kinsey Goman

Strategic Planning and Management, R Henry Migliore

Techniques to Measure Ideas

Essential Management Checklists, Jeffrey P Davidson

Index